PRAISE FOR MINISTERING TO MILLENNIALS

Chris Martin has a heart for the Millennial generation and, in this book, it shows. Proving himself to be a capable guide navigating through all the statistics about the millennials, Chris combines current research, biblical theology, and a missionary mindset in order to help us all become more effective in reaching this generation for Jesus.

Dr. Trevin Wax
Bible and Reference Publisher Broadman & Holman, author of *This Is Our Time: Everyday Myths in Light of the Gospel*

So often we see analysis of millennials from those on the outside looking in. But this is not that. Ministry to Millennials is written by a millennial about his generation. Although this book would be helpful for all people to read, pastors and parents will uniquely benefit from Chris's insights. This generation is large and diverse, if you desire to serve, love, and reach this generation with the gospel, you'll be glad you read this book.

Trillia Newbell
Author of *Enjoy and Fear and Faith*

Leading across generations is challenging today, but in *Ministering to Millenials*, Chris Martin provides practical tips on making things easier and bridging the gap. This book will help pastors and leaders of all kinds better understand the Millenial generation, and how to effectively lead them.

Brad Lomenick
Former President of Catalyst, author of *H3 Leadership* and *The Catalyst Leader*

In *Ministering to Millennials*, Chris Martin provides a resource that I recommend for any church or ministry hoping to engage the largest generation in American history. He provides clear steps for pastors and church leaders to better understand, reach, and equip Millennials while keeping the gospel of Jesus Christ at the center. Read this book, and do not let your fear of Millennials prevent you from sharing the gospel with them and discipling them.

Dr. Ed Stetzer
Billy Graham Distinguished Chair, Wheaton College

Millennials represent the most diverse generation in American history, and are often wrongly criticized as lazy, entitled, and narcissistic. Rather than joining this chorus of criticism, in Ministering to Millennials, Martin seeks to equip the church to understand and engage this generation with the gospel.

Dr. Russell Moore
President, Ethics and Religious Liberty Commission

As a pretty stereotypical Baby Boomer (born 1959) I've had a great interest in the Millennials. First, our kids are of this generation and married to people who are as well. Second, both in my academic career and as a pastor to young professionals I'm hip-deep in Millennials all the time. Beyond this, God has given me a deep passion for the next generation, of whom Millennials represent the lion's share. That's why I'm so happy to commend this book by my friend Chris Martin. Everybody seems to want to be an expert on generations it seems, but not everyone wants to pay the price to study them with precision. Chris has done just that. This is the generation most churches are not reaching, but I can tell you from research and personal, pastoral experience they are very reachable, and more than that form a potential army of missional believers to impact the church and culture better than those before them. Read this, get to know some Millennials, and invest in this vital generation.

Dr. Alvin L. Reid

Senior Professor of Evangelism and Student Ministry/Bailey Smith Chair of Evangelism, Southeastern Baptist Theological Seminary, and Pastor to Young Professionals, Richland Creek Community Church

MINISTERING TO MILLENNIALS

UNDERSTAND. REACH. EQUIP.

CHRIS MARTIN

Ministering to Millennials: Understand. Reach. Equip.

ISBN 978-1-948022-02-6

Rainer Publishing
www.RainerPublishing.com
Spring Hill, TN

Printed in the United States of America

To my wife, Susie:
Like all of life, writing this book would have
been more difficult and less joyful without
you. I love you, and you love me so well.

CONTENTS

FOREWORD

I like Chris Martin.

He is an introvert like me. We love not talking to each other. We don't worry about awkward conversations when we happen to get on an elevator together. We may grunt a few syllables, but then we move into blissful silence.

But I like Chris for more reasons than his introversion. I like him because he knows his generation. He understands the Millennials. He is more than a casual observer. He is a researcher of the highest caliber, not just a numbers and stats researcher, but a keen observer of all things Millennials.

Indeed, when I want to know the attitudes of Christian Millennials, I look to Chris. When I want to get a deeper understanding of the non-Christian Millennials, I look to Chris. When I really want to know how they think, how they work, how they are motivated, and how they will respond, I look to Chris.

In your hands is an incredibly valuable tome about the Millennial generation. Frankly, you will find few resources with the kind of insights you are about to read. You will be amazed at his prescient knowledge, his thoughtful insights, and his fair treatment of a generation that has been analyzed, categorized, and stereotyped.

By the way, Chris works for me at LifeWay Christian Resources. I know him in that context as well. From day one at LifeWay, he has made a great impression and far exceeded any high expectations we may have had of him. If the entitled Millennial myth had any traction with us, he destroyed that fable quickly.

If you are leading a church, you have the right book to learn about the Millennials. If you are in the business world, you have the right book to learn about the Millennials. If you are a student of generational studies, you have the right book about the Millennials.

But, even if you are none of the above, you have the right book. You see, this book is a clear mirror of our society and culture today. It offers insights even the most casual reader would enjoy and greatly benefit from.

I am thankful for Chris Martin. I am thankful for this book. But, above all, I am thankful for the heart of the man behind this book. You are about to enter the world of the Millennials from the perspective of one of the most gifted and insightful men I have ever known. He is a gift to many of us. And because of his relative youth, I pray he will be that gift for many years to come.

Thom S. Rainer

President and CEO

LifeWay Christian Resources

www.ThomRainer.com

— INTRODUCTION

What if I told you that you could fill your church with Millennials in three easy steps?

I'd be lying, that's what.

What if I recommended you simply add some mood lighting to your worship, order some organic, fair trade coffee for your baristas, wear lots of plaid on stage, and *then* you'd have Millennials lining up to worship Jesus?

Nope. Still lying.

But what if I told you that by considering cultural trends and proclaiming the gospel, your church may have more opportunities to reach and equip Millennials than you do now?

Now we might be onto something.

Ministry to Millennials isn't magic. Among those born between 1980 and 2000,[1] ideological and cultural diversity is more pervasive than ever in American history. This complicates ministry to Millennials. The relative continuity between Baby Boomers (1940_1960) and Gen Xers (1960_1980) is absent between Gen Xers and Millennials.[2] As a result, Boomers and Gen Xers may need a bit of guidance as they attempt to understand and minister to a generation that seems foreign, both literally and virtually.

Millennials make up the largest generation in American history, and to faithfully steward the gospel, pastors and church leaders must attempt to understand them, reach those who don't believe, and equip those who do.

But before we go any further, we have to deal with the elephant in the room.

ISN'T GENERATIONAL STUDY HOGWASH?

If you're like me, you're hesitant when it comes to this sort of book. Before I started studying Millennials, I thought,

"Generational study is basically like horoscope reading, right? You just look at a bunch of data and make it mean whatever you want it to mean."

Unfortunately, that can be true.

A common concern about studying Millennials, or conducting generational study as a whole, is the inability to provide precision or clarity. Most people see generational analysis as researchers and writers making statistics do gymnastics before their eyes and calling it "analysis." I share this concern, yet here I am writing this book for you. Why?

The concern that generational analysis is not *precise* is legitimate. That is, if you're looking for *precision*. But generational analysis, especially as it pertains to a generation as diverse as Millennials, is not always conducted for the purpose of providing precision. In this book we will conduct generational analysis not to provide precision but to recognize and minister in its absence.

Paul Taylor and Scott Keeter, editors of Pew Research Center's first landmark Millennials study in 2010, *Millennials: Confident. Connected. Open to Change*, write at the outset, "We are mindful that there are as many differences in attitudes, values, behaviors and lifestyles within a generation as there are between generations. But we believe this reality does not diminish the value of generational analysis; it merely adds to its richness and complexity."[3]

This book is written not to give pastors two or three generalities upon which they may base their Millennial ministry—such counsel is unwise and unhelpful. This book is written to help pastors and church members recognize and minister among the diversity of the Millennial generation.

So, if you're looking for the silver bullet to woo young people to fill your church, you'll be disappointed. But if you're looking for a careful analysis of Millennial trends and ways that may help you reach and equip them, you'll be encouraged.

As I've analyzed dozens of Millennial studies the last four years, I've concluded that only one generalization can be made about the Millennial generation: *it is too diverse to generalize*. I will repeat this throughout the book. It's too important to forget.

Millennials make up the largest generation in America's history, and as the United States continues to uphold its reputation as a "melting pot," this trend will only continue.

Many of those who conduct generational study and attempt to apply it to their selected field of interest treat the data like their local Chinese buffet. They peruse the spread of Millennial data, picking and choosing the tastiest bits of statistics as they lollygag down the line, and eventually they sit down at their tables and crunch the numbers to their liking. The problem is, result is often as undesirable as the result of eating at your local Chinese buffet, if you know what I mean.

To avoid bloating this book with unhelpful methods, I offer these three commitments to you, the reader:

I will not be definitive when the data is not definitive.

When doing generational study in a book like this, or on my blog every week, it's tempting to make confident statements that favor whatever point I'm trying to make. These usually come in the form of superlatives _ words like "most" or "highest" or "smartest" and the like. Some superlatives are necessary proper in generational study, particularly when supported by data.

For instance, if I wanted to say, "The Millennial generation has the most selfie-takers of any generation." My superlative is appropriate because, according to Pew, 55 percent of Millennials say they have shared a selfie, compared to 24 percent of Gen Xers, and 9 percent of Boomers. But if I wanted to say, "Millennials are the most self-centered generation in American history," my superlative would be a bit out of place. How do we quantify "self-centeredness" in a way that allows us to compare the self-centeredness of generations? We can't. One could say that Millennials are prone to self-centeredness because of the rate at which they take selfies and promote themselves on social media, but even so, this is not definitive.

I will avoid using superlatives without statistics to show you it's true.

I will hold the data with an open hand.

As I wrote above, I've analyzed dozens of Millennial studies over the years. These studies come in all shapes and sizes. Pew Research Center releases massive troves of data like their *Millennials in Adulthood* study, and organizations like the Public Religion Research Institute (PRRI) release smaller, more focused surveys like their *How Race and Religion Shape Millennial Attitudes on Sexuality and Reproductive Health* study. Because of the wealth of data that exists surrounding the Millennial generation, it is important to hold the numbers with an open hand.

For many of the same reasons we should be uncomfortable making sweeping superlative statements about Millennials; we should also be wary of holding on to just one or two data sets as the foundation of our conclusions. To only consult one study or to hang our hats on one number is akin to proof-texting a theological principle with only one verse or passage of Scripture. As one consults the full counsel of God in developing his theology, so must we consult as much data as possible in our study of Millennials. Sometimes we will only be able to consult a study or two, and that will have to suffice. But we will analyze as much data as is available on a subject before making significant conclusions about it.

As the author, I commit to you, the reader, that I will hold the data with an open hand. I have no agenda. I have nothing to prove. I just want to help.

I will suggest, not command.

Commitments 1 and 2 address how I will attempt to handle data with care. This third and final commitment pertains more to the ministry application that this book uniquely provides. All the data and surveys I access for this book are available to you. I have no special subscriptions or research assistants accessing this data from the vaults of research companies. You could access any of this data for free online or in books, and I am more than happy to provide my bibliography to you.

What makes this book unique is the ministry application in the "Reaching" and "Equipping" sections. In these sections I will pass on to you some of the insights of learned from a decade of teaching Millennials in the local church. Since I started teaching elementary-age Sunday school when I was barely a teenager, up to working with high school and college students today, I've kept track of what works and what doesn't.

I won't "command" you to do this or that. However, as a Millennial who has taught Millennials in the local church for ten years, I hope to take my experiences, the experiences of others, the knowledge of others, and the data presented throughout and suggest ways you can share the gospel and lead the local church with Millennials in mind.

WHY SHOULD WE CARE ABOUT MILLENNIALS?

Millennials: everyone on the internet writes about them, and it seems like no one can stand them. What's the point of studying Millennials anyway? Aren't they just a bunch of entitled 20-somethings who think they invented the phone they bought with their parents' money?

What's the point? Why should we care about Millennials?

The answer to that question is both simple and complex. The reason for understanding Millennials varies, depending on who *you* are. So, here are the reasons to study Millennials for a few different types of people who may be reading:

Pastors and church leaders, it's important for us to understand Millennials because...

It is our God-given duty to reach this generation with the gospel and serve alongside Millennials in the local church. When God called us to ministry, whether vocational or voluntary, he knew beforehand whom we would reach and equip. Millennials are normal, American people who just happen to be born in a 20-year period of time that is a bit different than the two previous 20-year periods.

In 2016 Millennials overtook Gen Xers as the largest generation in America's workforce, and they have overtaken Baby Boomers as the largest generation in American history.

They are a force to be reckoned with. Perhaps, you're intimidated, nervous, overwhelmed by Millennials. You wish they would take their selfie sticks and go home. It's exhausting to attempt to engage a people group you struggle to understand. Regardless of how we feel about Millennials, e need to love them because Christ has commanded us to love them. Pastors and church leaders, if we are to steward well the gifts and calling God has given us, we must care about Millennials because they are created in the image of God and they are a mission field of gospel opportunity.

Parents, it's important for you to understand Millennials because...

They're probably your children! If they aren't your children, they're likely your co-workers. If you're a 35-or-under parent, you're a Millennial yourself and you can move on to the next section.

I'm a Millennial born in 1990, and my parents are right on the line between Boomers and Gen Xers, born in 1960 and 1965. It's important for parents to understand Millennials because you have to interact with them on a regular basis, either in the home or in the office.

I don't have kids yet, but I know the biblical priority for parents to pass the faith on to their children. Parents of Millennials, show your kids the unconditional love of Jesus even when it's hard. Often, to best love people, you must work hard to understand them. Millennials want to be understood by their parents as much as anyone does, even when it seems like they don't.

Millennials, it's important for you to understand Millennials because...

You are one, quite simply. Why not fulfill the Millennial stereotype and care about yourself more than anyone else?

But seriously, cultural engagement is a responsibility of all Christians. If we truly want the best for others, and if we truly want to see people flourish, we need to care about them. Millennials need to care about the salvation and well-being of their own generation.

For the same reason it is important for Western missionaries to train and equip Asian pastors to shepherd the people who come to Christ in the mission field, it is important for Boomer and Gen X pastors to train and equip Millennial Christians to shepherd their peers. Millennials, we know the quirks and quandaries of our generation better than anyone; this is a responsibility we mustn't take lightly.

In sum, everyone should care about Millennials because everyone has to interact with them. Whether you're a businessperson managing Millennials at the office, a parent raising Millennials at home, or a pastor shepherding Millennials in your community, this generation of young people needs to be understood, reached with the gospel, and equipped so that we may faithfully fulfill the Great Commission us.

Millennials aren't special_they aren't holier or cooler than anyone else. They just have quirks that other generations didn't, largely thanks to the influence of the internet, and it can be tough for older generations to connect as a result. That's why I'm writing this book.

WHO ARE MILLENNIALS, REALLY?

Originally called "Generation Y" because they followed a generation called "Generation X," Millennials are typically defined as those who were born between 1980-2000, though there is no consensus on the range, particularly when it comes to the end of the generation.

As one would expect, those Millennials born closer to 1980 are prone to be more aligned with Gen Xers, and those born around and after 1990 are more like the generation to come after Millennials, called "Generation Z" (for now).

In Part One, "Understanding," we'll dig into data that gives us a more detailed description of Millennials. First, though, we need to dismantle some stereotypes and identify the lowest common denominator, where much of what makes Millennials different finds its root.

Abandon Millennial Stereotypes

Stereotypes are always built on a kernel of perceived truth, but if there's ever been a generation you would be unwise to stereotype, it'd be this one. Like I said before, we should avoid using generalities when it comes to Millennials except for one: Millennials are too diverse to be generalized.

Within American evangelicalism today, Millennials are often seen as 20-somethings who want to mooch off of their parents, sleeping around and wasting their college degrees on coffee shop jobs as they attempt to extend adolescence and delay real life as long as possible. Contrary to what many people think, not every Millennial is a lazy 24-year-old male living in his parents' basement, subsisting on a steady diet of Mountain Dew and Pizza Rolls and blowing his paycheck on the newest video games. That stereotype is worth considering, but it is just that: a stereotype. A few people fit it; a lot of people don't.

Before ministering to Millennials, it's wise to dismantle the stereotypes that annoy you when you think of young people. Stereotypes can be problematic because they can lead to unnecessary assumptions that may cloud you from acknowledging realities that don't fit your stereotype. For instance, holding to the stereotype that Millennials live with their parents because they're lazy may keep you from sympathizing with a Millennial in your church who's living in his parents' basement because he can't find a job or is carrying a massive load of student debt. Further, Millennials are stereotyped as being addicted to their phones, but perhaps your granddaughter keeps checking her phone at the dinner table not because she's being mentioned on Twitter but because her boss expects her to check her email at all times of the day.

If you're really trying to reach young people, you would do well to clear your mind of all the stereotypes. As true as many of them may be in certain contexts, they tend to hurt more than they help. I don't imagine the Baby Boomer Christians don't like being stereotyped as the cash cows of the church who will keep tithing as long as we keep the organ on the stage. In the same way, it's safe to assume Millennials don't like being characterized as lazy bums.

Identify the Lowest Common Denominator

When it comes to understanding what makes Millennials different, it's helpful to find the lowest common denominator, or that one common thread that runs throughout all the intricacies of what makes Millennials worth studying. What makes Millennials different from Gen Xers and Boomers? It's the internet. The internet is the lowest common denominator among a myriad of differences between Millennials and the generations of Americans that have come before them.

Millennials are different because they typed their first essays on Mac computers, not IBM Selectric typewriters.

They accessed encyclopedias online, not in the library.

They talked to their friends on AOL Instant Messenger, not party phone lines.

To be fair, the internet existed in some form at least a decade or two before Millennials barged onto the scene of human history, but no one grew up with it in the family room or in their pockets until we did.

Just think about it for a moment. Think about everything that irks you about Millennials: everything that they value, the ways they communicate, form ideas, evaluate ethics, and interact with culture. The interconnectedness provided by the internet revolutionized how Millennials developed. For older Millennials, those born closer to 1980, the internet didn't seep into their psychological development until the end of high school and the beginning of college. For Millennials born toward the middle of the generation, like me, around 1990, many had access to at least dial-up internet in elementary school, and perhaps had even graduated to something like DSL by middle school. When '80s kids hit college, they were learning how to log on to AOL. When early '90s kids hit college, they were laughing at cat videos and binge-watching Netflix. That's a big difference even *within* the generation.

Even further down the line, consider the youngest Millennials born in the late '90s (whom some researchers don't even consider Millennials). These kids, just now hitting adulthood, have Snapchatted and Instagrammed their way through high school.

Scary.

As a future parent, I shudder to think what technology will be around when *my* kids are learning how to drive.

As I was outlining this book, I debated writing a chapter on the internet, but I found it more prudent to mention it here in the introduction and weave it throughout the book because, quite frankly, I believe the internet undergirds a lot of what we're going to be looking at as it pertains to understanding, reaching, and equipping Millennials. Because the internet is this generation's lowest common denominator, I will connect many of the topics we unpack throughout the book back to it.

WHAT SHOULD WE DO ABOUT MILLENNIALS?

The first thing we have to do is not freak out.

But what about beyond that? This book is broken down into three basic parts to explain just that, below are summaries of those three parts with one overarching action as well.

Pray

Before anything else, take time to pray. I write about this on my blog often, and sometimes it feels forced and kitschy, but I am constantly reminded of the power and importance of prayer in the life of the Christian. Before you set out to try to connect with young people in your community, share the gospel with them, and invite them to your church, you must pray.

Working to reach Millennials is important, but if you aren't careful, out of desperation you'll start submitting to the will of Millennials before you submit to the will of God. Prayer protects against that. Also, pastors, remember: Millennials are not the future of your church. Disciples are the future of your church.

Work to reach Millennials, but only because they're next in line. Before you know it, it'll be time to reach their children. The job of the local church is not to make disciples of Millennials. It's to make disciples of the nations.

After some serious time of prayer, work to do the next three things.

Understand them.

I played a lot of video games growing up, and I still do. My favorite video game of all time is the original Pokémon Red/Blue game on GameBoy Color.

The game came out when I was in the third grade, and I spent countless hours catching and training my Pokémon. I have played almost every Pokémon since the original. No matter how many Pokémon they add or new features they add to the game, there is one key to success: understand what types of Pokémon are strong and weak against other types of Pokémon. Fire Pokémon are weak against water-type and strong against grass-type. Rock-type Pokémon are strong against electric-type and weak against water-type. Ultimately, Pokémon is just a really complicated game of rock, paper, scissors.

The better you understand different types of Pokémon, the more effective your strategy will be. In the same way, the better you understand Millennials, the more effective your strategies for reaching and equipping them will be. The gospel is the power of God to save, and it can overcome our poor strategy, but why not give it our best shot?

Reach them.

After working to better understand Millennials, we'll look at how we might reach unbelieving Millennials with the gospel. This part of the book focuses on how the local church interacts with Millennials who are not yet Christians. It may help for us to look a Millennials as an unreached people group of sorts, taking a step back from Millennial culture, looking at it like a new mission field, studying it and how the gospel is most effectively shared in it.

We need to take what we learn about Millennials in the "Understanding" section and apply it to evangelism and working among the unreached Millennials in our communities. We'll work together to figure out how to do that.

Equip them.

Finally, in the last part of this book we'll work to figure out the most effective ways to equip and work alongside Millennials for the advance of the gospel and the Great Commission work Jesus has given us. We'll take the values we learned about in the "Understanding" section and demonstrate how those universal Millennial values apply in the setting of the local church.

Like I said before, Millennials aren't "special" or better

than any other generations in any way. They are just a little different, which makes ministering to them a little foggy. Throughout this book we'll work not to clear the fog, but we'll work to learn to navigate it. Let's learn together.

SECTION

ONE

UNDERSTANDING

1/ **DIVERSITY**

ort Wayne, Indiana, is the second-largest city in Indiana and is nestled in the far northeast corner of the state, about an hour south of Michigan and twenty minutes west of Ohio. It is home to a substantial Amish population and boasts minor league baseball and hockey teams, a couple of shopping malls, and three major hospital networks. It is also where my wife and I grew up. When one thinks of a diverse city, Fort Wayne, Indiana doesn't come to mind. Cities like New York, Los Angeles, or Miami are *known* for their diversity, and on the surface, the most diverse feature of Fort Wayne is its rich Native American history. But the "City of Churches," as it has been called since the late 1800s, is quite diverse.

Fort Wayne is located at the intersection of three rivers: the Maumee, the St. Joseph, and the St. Marys. whose convergence all but demanded a city be built there. In the eighteenth century this a recipe for diversity a sort of cosmopolitan hub along well-traveled waterways, attracting people from all walks of life—Americans both Native and new.

Even today, Fort Wayne is becoming increasingly diverse. The high school my wife attended is home to over a dozen languages and made up of 51 percent non-white students. The city is also home to a significant Burmese population because of a refugee resettlement program—it is currently home to the largest population of Burmese in the United States.

When I think of the increasing diversity of my hometown, I think of how Millennials, and even younger generations to follow them, are increasing the diversity of the entire country. Without knowing any better, a mid-sized midwestern town like Fort Wayne, Indiana would not be considered a diverse city. But it is, and it is because America is becoming more diverse on the whole. As more and more people of different races immigrate to the United States, Millennials and the generations to come after them will turn this country into a minority-majority land, and that's good.

RACIAL DIVERSITY

Racial diversity is a determining factor of the Millennial generation. When I am asked to generalize the Millennial generation, I often say the only generalization we can make about Millennials is that they are too diverse to generalize. Millennials are diverse in a number of ways, one of which is racially.

The Millennial generation is, to this point, the most racially diverse generation in American history. Pew Research Center reported in its landmark *Millennials in Adulthood* study that 43 percent of Millennial adults are non-white.[4] Even more remarkable, approximately 50 percent of newborns in America today are non-white.[5] Millennials are more diverse than any generation to come before them, but they are giving birth to even more diversity, so their children will make up a generation even more diverse than their own.

Baby Boomers, defined by Pew Research Center as those born between 1946 and 1964, are the whitest generation in America—75 percent of them are white, which is higher than the national average of 61.6 percent.[6] Millennials, however, are only 55.8 percent white, three percentage points below the national average, making them the least white generation in America.

Even the Millennial minority population is more diverse than the Boomer minority population. Most of the 25 percent of Boomers who are not white are black, which is to say, the majority of Boomer minorities are black. However, this is not so among Millennials. Nearly 30 percent of all Millennials are Hispanic, Asian, or those identifying as two or more races.[7] Cities like Chicago, Los Angeles, and Miami have been referred to as "melting pot" cities, where people of all different backgrounds live, work, and play. In the same way, the entire Millennial generation is a "melting pot" generation, made up of not only one or two major races, but a handful of them.

While its racial diversity is central to its identity, Millennial diversity goes beyond racial differences. The most racially diverse generation in American history is also incredibly diverse ideologically.

IDEOLOGICAL DIVERSITY

The confused spirituality of Millennials will be examined in chapter 3, but because here it should be noted that 58 percent of Millennials say they believe and are absolutely certain about their belief in God, as opposed to 69 percent of Gen Xers and 73 percent of Boomers.

What about non-religious ideologies? Political ideology among Millennials is quite diverse, and, like their religious beliefs, quite ambiguous. I am not a political strategist, but I can imagine it is quite frustrating to try to market a particular candidate to a generation of Americans who are unwilling to identify with a political party no matter who they may ultimately vote for when the time comes.

As of 2014, 50 percent of Millennials identify as politically "Independent," 27 percent identify as "Democrat," and 17 percent as "Republican." Ten years earlier, in 2004, only 38 percent of Millennials identified as Independent. It appears that Millennials are becoming less committed to a particular side of the two-party-dominated system currently in place in American politics.

Why?

Truthfully, there are many possible reasons. Perhaps Millennials are fed up with political dysfunction, which, correctly or incorrectly, is often seen as rooted in the constant, vicious warring between Republicans and Democrats. Many Millennials find parts about each party attractive and repulsive, and the parts they find repulsive are often strong enough to repel them from identifying as a member of that party.

For example, Millennials who believe in the pro-life platform of Republicans may be motivated to vote for a Republican politician but may hesitate to call themselves a "Republican" because they find the party's stance on immigration offensive and unhelpful. Or, on the other side, Millennials may appreciate the Democratic Party's work to stop climate change and may vote for a Democratic politician but may balk at calling themselves a "Democrat" because they believe marriage is designed to be between one man and one woman.

Millennials, in an attempt to avoid being misunderstood, will avoid calling themselves "Republicans" or "Democrats" unless they are ready and willing to defend a majority of the party's platform. Thus, because many Millennials do not align with either party on a majority of its platform, they are hesitant to label themselves with a party name and instead may opt for more ideological labels like "Conservative," "Progressive," "Libertarian," or other such terms.

HOW DOES MILLENNIALS' DIVERSITY AFFECT MINISTRY TO MILLENNIALS?

Pastors and church leaders, as we work to understand Millennials in hopes of reaching them with the gospel and equipping them for ministry, we must understand that generalizations and stereotypes will be unhelpful and may ultimately handicap our ministry, no matter how well intentioned we may be.

Years ago, communities were more homogenous than they are today and young people tended to reflect the beliefs and values of the communities in which they were raised. This is no longer the case. In 1950, 90 percent of Americans were white; in 2010, only 72 percent of Americans were white. *All of America* is becoming more diverse, not just major urban areas.

Urban centers have always been known to host a diversity of races and ideologies. However, with the Millennial generation has come a diversity of backgrounds and values to rural and suburban areas. The cosmopolitan nature of urban centers has bled into suburbia and beyond. A young man growing up in rural Tennessee in the 1950s would likely believe much the same way his parents did, interacting with people who largely look and think like him. This is no longer the case, largely due to the internet (on that later), but also due to increased racial and ideological diversity.

As a diversity of backgrounds and ideals characterize our communities, pastors and church leaders must be ready and willing to engage with young people who look and think differently than they do. Toward that end, here are three postures pastors and church leaders should adopt.

A POSTURE OF HUMILITY

Rick Warren, pastor of Saddleback Church, writes in his book *The Purpose Driven Life*, "True humility is not thinking less of yourself; it is thinking of yourself less."[8] Humility is not about self-hate as much as it is about caring more about the needs of others than our own needs.

When it comes to living in an American culture that is increasingly diverse in many ways, understanding Millennials, reaching them with the gospel, and equipping them for Great Commission work will require a measure of Christ-like humility that puts the interests of others before our own.

What might this look like?

One of the most common exercises in humility is being willing to repent for sin. Doing ministry across generational lines is not easy. Misunderstandings happen. Toes are stepped on. Unwanted changes are made out of necessity. In short: multi-generational church ministry almost always includes conflict; this is especially true as cultures, races, and diverse ideologies mix together. Humility is, as much as we would like to dig in and figure out a way to prove we are right, apologizing when we see we have sinned against a brother or sister in Christ.

A pastor or church leader who acts in humility will approach Millennials (or anyone, for that matter) in such a way that says, "I know how I see this, but I know that Millennials may see it differently." This posture of humility enables us to pursue the following two postures.

A POSTURE OF LISTENING

Listening is difficult . . . for me, anyway. I'm a talker, and in more situations than I should, I tend to think I have the best solution for the problem at hand. I can be a bad listener. But, my wife would attest, this is an area that has been sanctified_at least in part_by our marriage.

Listening is important when it comes to working with young people, and in this case Millennials, because listening communicates, "I think your perspective is valuable." And really, when it comes down to it, listening is an act of love. Millennials, as much as anyone, want to be heard and loved. Navigating the diversity of Millennials will require us to listen because we are going to want to learn about them, which leads to the third and final posture.

A POSTURE OF LEARNING

A posture of humility plus a posture of listening equals a posture of learning. In order to learn, one must be humble enough to be silent and listen to others. But not all learning requires us to listen to others. In the internet age, almost any factual argument can be solved by a 30-second Google search. Wonder what movie you've seen that actress in before? Google it. Curious about how long it would take to sail around the world? Google it. In this way, learning in the twenty-first century is easy_it's just a few finger taps away.

But interpersonal learning, learning about who people are and how they work, cannot be Googled or otherwise solved by the internet (despite what social media would have us believe). Learning about people—how they think, work, and feel—is a slow task that often feels more like slogging through the mud than it does sprinting on a track.

Pastors and church leaders, if we truly want to understand Millennials, we must be willing to learn from them. Learning from Millennials can be difficult for older generations because it requires Gen Xers or Boomers to acknowledge that a group of people younger than them has insight they do not have. This is uncomfortable, but it is vital to understanding Millennials and reaching them with the gospel.

Look at the relationship between Timothy and Paul, who tells Timothy in 1 Timothy that he ought not let anyone despise him for his youth. Paul was a mighty man of God, but to think it was easy for him to disciple young Timothy is silly. Young people, whether they be Millennials or those even younger, cannot be avoided because of their youth. Harness their youth for the kingdom of God.

Are you unsure of why Millennials value what they do? Are you confused by the way Millennials think about work or family? Reconciling your confusion is quite simple; it only requires a humble willingness to listen to and learn from a Millennial or two.

However, as the saying goes, just because it's simple does not mean it will be easy. It is unnatural to learn from someone who has less life experience than you. But, when your goal is to better understand this group of people, learning directly from the source is a sign of wisdom and maturity. Listening to Millennials will help you better reach and equip a group of people in desperate need of the gospel.

The important practice of listening is not limited to our ministry to Millennials. It is true whenever trying to learn from people who are different than us in any way. For instance, it is wise to learn from a Brazilian about Brazilian life and culture in order to better reach Brazilians with the gospel. For this same reason, we must not scoff at the idea of learning from a Millennial about Millennial life and culture in order to better reach Millennials with the gospel.

ANYTHING BUT MONOLITHIC

The racial diversity of Millennials described above leads to cultural diversity, which, in turn, leads to a diversity of values. Millennials are anything but monolithic in a myriad of ways, and before you continue reading this book, you must understand that. Nothing in this book is universally applicable. Any generalizations in this book are just that—generalizations—and are going to be incorrect at times.

However, while diversity can be scary and difficult to navigate, pastors and church leaders can embark on better understanding, reaching, and equipping Millennials when they adopt postures of humility, listening, and learning.

2/ **AUTHENTICITY**

One night when I was in middle school, my family was sitting around the dinner table, peacefully eating one of my mom's many delicious meals, when my three-years-younger brother took the last roll out of the basket because he knew I wanted it. He had already had his share, and I hadn't had as many as he, so I kicked him under the table. Like a typical little brother, he tattled on me, and my parents sent me to my room as punishment.

Twenty or thirty minutes later, my mom told me I could come down from my room and finish my dinner, "But first," she said, "You need to apologize to your brother." Having zero remorse for my (in my mind) totally appropriate pursuit of justice, I sat for a moment deciding what to do. "Ok," I said, "Kyle, I am sorry . . . I didn't shove that roll down your throat." Flabbergasted at the abrupt turn of events, my mother dispatched me back to my room for what was certainly the rest of the night.

On display at the dinner table that evening was more than adolescent disobedience—it was *authenticity*, albeit warped and sinful. I was not at all sorry for assaulting my brother for stealing a roll that was rightfully mine, and despite my mom's reconciliatory desire for me to apologize, I refused to fake my remorse. To my 13-year-old self, being stubbornly honest about this grave injustice was worth an evening finding ways to occupy myself in my room. The pride-shaming act of faking an apology to my little brother was worse in my middle-school mind than disobeying my parents and sinning before God. I cared about authenticity more than I cared about obedience. In this moment, "authenticity" wasn't as much about my identity as it was about my attitude. Authenticity goes beyond our attitudes and day-to-day actions. Authenticity is about who we are in the core of our being.

Millennials value "authenticity," but authenticity can be a rather vague concept. What is "authenticity," really, and how do Millennials understand it?

A BRIEF EXPLORATION INTO "AUTHENTICITY"

The term "authenticity" is understood by different people in different ways. The primary definition for "authentic" according to Merriam-Webster is, "worthy of acceptance or belief as conforming to or based on fact." An example sentence for this usage is, "That painting is an authentic Van Gogh piece." Another definition Merriam-Webster provides is, "made or done in the same way as an original." The common appearance of this definition is in regard to food, like, "I prefer authentic Mexican food rather than Tex-Mex." However, one of the final definitions Merriam-Webster gives is perhaps the most common usage of "authentic" in twenty-century America, "true to one's own personality, spirit, or character." To an almost-nauseating degree, "authentic" or "authenticity," is used like this, "Just be authentic—be true to yourself."

To be fair, there is value in this understanding of authenticity. It is exhausting to force positivity at all times or to attempt to be someone we're not. "Being true to yourself" sounds cheesy and self-aggrandizing, but, if we're honest, it's better than the alternative _not_ being true to ourselves could be deceptive and malicious.

This self-realization form of authenticity is what Millennials value. For Millennials, "idealistic authenticity" is the absence of a façade and the presence of reality, however imperfect or broken that reality may be. The problem is, in a pursuit of this idealistic authenticity, many Millennials end up creating façades to feign authenticity. Creating a persona that is peddled as "authentic" actually ends up being more attractive than being _truly authentic_.

Millennials _say_ they care about authenticity more than they _actually_ care about authenticity, and this is perhaps clearest on the internet. The internet has benefitted us in countless ways: Amazon provides two-day shipping of just about anything we want, FaceTime allows us to have virtual face-to-face conversations with friends and family members around the world, and Airbnb provides us with cheaper lodging options than may be available through traditional hotels. These are just three of countless technologies made possible by the internet that make our lives easier in one way or another.

But the internet is a powerful beast. It is not just a tool that exists in reality—the internet is so comprehensive that it can parallel real life and create a pseudo-reality that exists alongside real life. Simply put: we can live lives on the internet that are very different than the lives we live off the internet.

Social media, in particular, enables this phenomenon. Social media has its benefits, but one of the many pitfalls of social media is that it enables us to create alternate realities—alternate personas—that ultimately do not represent who we are in our offline lives. I call this phenomenon "selective sharing." Social media allows us to selectively share who we are so that, intentionally or not, our flaws disappear or seem less prominent and problematic than they really are.

Social media, a tool that is theoretically supposed to *enhance* effective communication and social interaction, actually *hinders* effective communication and social interaction because the personas we create online are often inaccurate depictions of who we really are. One could make the case that social media creates many more obstacles in the pursuit of authentic, intimate relationships than it destroys.

This is where Millennials fumble "authenticity." Social media handicaps authentic relationships because who we are on social media does not accurately depict who we are in real life, even if we make no attempts at inaccurately representing ourselves online. Everything we post online is filtered. Unless we are constantly streaming every second of our days on Periscope or Facebook Live, who we are on social media is only a partial— and therefore inaccurate—representation of who we really are. This sort of subconscious filtering keeps us from sharing parts of ourselves that we would rather others not notice.

Throughout human history we have had the ability to look more important, secure, rich, happy, or attractive than we really are. This sort of deception is not a new phenomenon, but maintaining a façade of happiness in face-to-face interactions is much more difficult than maintaining that same façade online.

For instance, my wife is brilliant at noticing when I'm upset. I can try to hide it all I want, but if I'm mad, disappointed, annoyed, or compelled by just about any other sort of negative feeling, she identifies it immediately over the dinner table or in the car on the way home from work. But, my anger doesn't ooze out of my Instagram pictures, and my sadness doesn't proliferate my Twitter timeline. My friends who only know me through my social media platforms don't see when I get frustrated about work or when my wife and I have an argument. I don't try to misrepresent myself on social media, but by not sharing every part of my life, good or bad, I am unintentionally painting a false picture of who I actually am.

Millennials misunderstand authenticity, in part, because we fall into the trap that our online interactions are representative of reality. These interactions are actually representative of a false reality that runs parallel to the true reality.

Another way Millennials' value of "authenticity" may be tainted is this: Millennials' love for authenticity has ultimately led to an acceptance of brokenness that is unhealthy, especially within the church. This is the dark side of the "be true to yourself" brand of authenticity. "Be true to yourself" or "Be who you were meant to be" are common refrains, especially among those attempting to influence young people. In *The Gifts of Imperfection*, author and renowned TED-talk speaker Brené Brown writes, "Authenticity is the daily practice of letting go of who we think we're supposed to be and embracing who we are."[9] This is inspiring enough to squeeze a "Hallelujah" out of an atheist, but I wouldn't want a serial killer taking Ms. Brown's advice here. For my nerd readers out there, Obi-Wan Kenobi, Jedi knight and mentor to Anakin Skywalker (before he became Darth Vader), once said, "You must do what you feel is right." That sounds nice, unless, of course, you are Anakin Skywalker and you feel like killing all of the younglings in the Jedi temple. That would be when this advice goes awry.

Millennials' understanding of authenticity as "being true to yourself" is problematic because it often demands that we be content with who we are despite how messed up we are. This understanding of authenticity is damning because it tells us, "Who you are is good enough; you don't need anything or anyone else," when, in fact, we are in desperate need of a Savior! Authenticity as "being true to yourself" assumes that who we are is worth being true to. It squashes any need for self-improvement, personal growth, or, in Christian terms, sanctification. If we pursue authenticity in hopes of being true to who we are, we put ourselves on a path that leads us to believe we do not need a Savior because we are fine *just how we are*.

Renowned philosopher Charles Taylor writes in *A Secular Age* that the "secular age" really ought to be called the "Age of Authenticity."[10] He defines the "Age of Authenticity" like this:

> I mean the understanding of life which emerges with the Romantic expressivism of the late-eighteenth century, that each one of us has his/her own way of realizing our humanity, and that it is important to find and live out one's own, as against surrendering to conformity with a model imposed on us from outside, by society, or the previous generation, or religious or political authority.[11]

In modern American culture, especially among young people, authenticity is all about being loyal to one's identity and inner self. More and more, the identities of young people _ Millennials included _ are being defined less by religion and patriotism and more by how well they imitate the style of Khloé Kardashian or the language of popular music.

The world settles for a cheap version of authenticity _ an authenticity that is ultimately dictated by who we *want* to be. Christianity tells a different story.

Christianity says that authenticity is rooted in *whose* we are, not who we want to be. Real authenticity is recognizing that our identity is not found in what we have done, but what has been done *for* us. Christians pursuing authenticity do not seek to be "true to themselves" but true to the One who has saved them, Jesus. The conflict between the Christian and secular definitions of "authenticity" comes because religion brings a moral and supernatural order that limits the self-expression at the heart of the secular pursuit of authenticity.

It's safe to say that when Millennials say they value "authenticity," this value spills over into their social and sexual values. These values are notable and must be considered by pastors and church leaders who hope to reach unbelieving Millennials with the gospel and equip believing Millennials to go gospel ministry.

SEX AND RELATIONSHIPS IN AN AGE OF AUTHENTICITY

An important feature of a generation determined to be "true to themselves" is sexual freedom. Millennials value sexual freedom—the ability to do whatever they want with their bodies in regards to sexuality—more than just about any generation in history, and that is shown by their views on sexuality, abortion, and otherwise. Statistics clearly show that Millennials are delaying marriage but not sex.

The delay of marriage is likely due to several factors, the primary of which are often identified as the pursuit of professional development and a hesitation birthed from the divorce culture of their parents. In true Millennial fashion, let's focus on sex first and marriage second.

SEX AND REPRODUCTIVE RIGHTS

A 2015 survey by the Public Religion Research Institute (PRRI) is a treasure trove of data regarding Millennials' attitudes toward sexuality and reproductive health. According to this survey, 88 percent of Millennials identify as heterosexual or straight, which is quite low. Likewise, 15 percent of Millennials say their understanding of their sexual orientation has changed since they were adolescents, which shows how culture has shifted Millennials' views on sexuality over the last decade or so. Regarding same-sex relationships, 35 percent of Millennials say that more gay and lesbian couples raising children is a good thing for society, according to Pew's *Millennials in Adulthood* study. According to that same study, 68 percent of Millennials support same-sex marriage, as opposed to just 55 percent of Gen Xers and 48 percent of Boomers. All of this is to say: Millennials have ever-changing views on sexuality that vary widely from those who came before them. What about their views on abortion and reproductive health?

Pew's *Millennials in Adulthood* study reports that 56 percent of Millennials say "Abortion should be legal in all or most cases," but according to the PRRI survey, 51 percent of them say abortion services should *not* be covered by health insurance. Eight percent of Millennial women report that they have had an abortion, and 36 percent of Millennials say that a close friend or family member has had an abortion.[12] However, while Millennials seem to have a disturbingly close relationship with abortion, the generation seems to be quite split about how they see the issue. While only 25 percent of Millennials identify as exclusively pro-life, only 27 percent of Millennials identify as exclusively pro-choice[13] This further shows the ideological divide among Millennials.

One of the saddest of these statistics is that 47 percent of births to women in the Millennial generation in 2012 were non-marital, or to an unmarried woman. That statistic tells us that just five years ago, almost *half* of children born to Millennial women were born into an unmarried and possibly single-parent home. It is a sad, staggering reality, despite the fact that, according to the same study Pew study, 58 percent of Millennials say that more children being raised by single parents is a bad thing for society. Heartbreaking. So, what about marriage? How do Millennials feel about the oldest relational institution in the history of humanity?

MARRIAGE MATTERS . . . OR DOES IT?

A long-running stereotype about I've seen about Millennials is that they don't want to get married. It is true that Millennials are delaying marriage, but the idea that Millennials don't want to get married simply isn't true on a broad scale. A 2014 report from the Clark Poll of Emerging adult shows that 69 percent of Millennials would like to be married eventually. But data also shows us that Millennials are getting married later: the average Millennial woman is approximately 27 years old when she weds, and the average Millennial man is 29 years old. Though most unmarried Millennials want to be married at some point, it is clear that few are actually in a hurry to do so.

This affects the way how local churches attempt to reach unbelieving Millennials with the gospel and how it equips believing Millennials to do gospel ministry. A sermon series on marriage that makes little or no mention of singles may be more off-putting to young people than in the past, and churches may want to consider creative, non-cliché ways to minister to the single Millennials who come to church.

My wife and I got married immediately after we graduated college, so I spent virtually no time in the church as a single, 20-something adult. But I know from simply talking to single friends that even the kindest, most well-intentioned churches can feel awkward for single people. Churches who wish to reach Millennials should consider how they might best serve and minister to single young people, and really the best way to do this is by asking them. Why would married church leaders try to guess about the needs of the single people in their churches when they could just take them to coffee and ask them? However we decide to serve the single people in our churches, we must saturate our ministries in the reconciling gospel of Jesus Christ because whatever unique needs single Millennials have are ultimately trumped by their needs for salvation and grace.

So, regardless of how "authenticity" may manifest itself in how Millennials think about sexuality, relationships, or otherwise, how do pastors and church leaders minister to a group of people who want to "be real" with one another?

HOW DOES MILLENNIALS' QUEST FOR AUTHENTICITY SHAPE HOW WE MINISTER TO THEM?

Though Millennial perspectives on "authenticity" are quite disparate, ministering to them in light of their quest for authenticity remains quite simple.

First, shatter the façade. In church life, this is most easily seen in how we interact with each other on Sunday mornings in between worship services. "Hey Cara! How is your week going?" Jenna asks. "Oh, it's been pretty good," Cara replies, deciding not to go into detail about how her third-grade classroom was one "He pushed me!" away from implosion.

This past year my wife and I moved to a different suburb of Nashville and joined a new church. It is only about six years old and is made up largely of Millennials—many of them college students from a local state university. As I have interacted with many of the Millennials in our church, one of the most common reasons they say they were attracted to this church in the first place is because they recognized that fake happiness is absent. "People here are real. They don't just act like life is great all the time," they say. Millennials know the world is broken as much as anyone else; they will not be fooled by a church full of Christians who act like everything is great all the time.

Millennials also value authenticity because they value *community*. It is difficult to build real, deep, lasting community with a group of people when everyone is firmly positioned behind their respective façades of happiness and perfection.

Second, show Millennials the cross does not void their unique personalities. The idea that identity and authenticity are ultimately rooted in Christ and what he has done for us will almost certainly repulse unbelieving Millennials in our communities. Because of this, it is important that we make clear that though Christ calls us to die to ourselves, we need not abandon who we are. A Christ-centered version of identity and authenticity does not mortify what makes us unique. A Christ-centered vision of identity and authenticity simply aligns what makes us unique with the mission of the cross— the reconciliation of humanity to God. Finding our identity in the gospel brings contented rest; creating an identity for ourselves brings fruitless exhaustion.

Third, show them how their personal hopes and dreams can align with the eternal perspective of the cross. In much the same way that the cross does not mortify our unique personalities, the cross need not mortify our hopes and dreams. Enrolling in medical school or pursuing a career in Major League Baseball need not be derailed when one seeks a Christ-centered authenticity. Finding one's authentic identity in Christ simply aligns the passions of our hearts and the goals of our lives with the Great Commission of Jesus Christ and his desire to reconcile all people to himself.

THE NECESSITY OF AUTHENTICITY

Do not quench the Millennial pursuit of authenticity, however misguided it may be. Simply show the Millennials in our churches and communities, with grace and humility, that true "authenticity" is about more than being true to who *we* are_it's about being true to the One who gave himself because of who we *cannot* be. Minister to Millennials by recognizing their hesitations about marriage and find ways to minister the gospel to them in their particular contexts. Remember that intentional, intimate gospel community cannot be achieved without authenticity. Millennials value this sort of community despite how uncomfortable it may be at times.

3/ **SPIRITUALITY**

I am generally bad about keeping up with friends from high school. I've lived away from Indiana for over four years now, and in the midst of trying to make new friends, I have, unfortunately, not been as good about keeping up with old ones as I like. But, I have been good about keeping up with a friend named Kurt (whose name I've altered for his privacy). Kurt and I were friends in high school but haven't seen each other since graduation.

However, through the magic of Facebook, we keep in touch.

Kurt grew up in a Catholic home but no longer follows the faith of his youth. Kurt is quite interested in matters of spirituality, but he doesn't attend church and doesn't ascribe to any single faith system. Kurt and I differ theologically, politically, philosophically, and otherwise, but we always manage to have constructive conversations about important, controversial topics. Kurt may pop up throughout this chapter as an example of a spiritual-but-not-religious Millennial.

Kurt and I do book exchanges and send each other videos or links to articles we think the other would find interesting. A while back Kurt sent me a video of Russell Brand talking about spiritual matters. Brand, if you're unaware, is an English entertainer. He's hosted a radio program, authored articles and books, and done stand-up comedy, but he is perhaps best known for his roles in movies like *Forgetting Sarah Marshall* and *Get Him to the Greek*. He is also known for his political activism and occasional spiritual discussions.

The video is eleven-minutes long; here's a selection of some of its more notable lines:

> "It's through spiritual practice that I've recognized my own impermanence, my own irrelevance, the fact that I'm just a person, shuffling through life."

"It's good to have access to the infinite consciousness that is available to all people, but, through the five senses, is delineated, keeping us trapped on a material plane."

"We are, by our nature, spiritual people."

"Within ourselves there is an infinite capacity for connection with all things."

"You can't define yourself in reference to other, external coordinates. You must define yourself internally, in your relationship with the higher entity. Think of yourself as a manifestation of some higher thing, some higher frequency."

"I choose to believe in God because I think what that is the recognition that there is divine beauty in all of us."

"I recognize the capacity in myself for selfishness, for lustfulness, for egotism, and because I recognize these qualities in myself, I would prefer a culture that did not celebrate, exacerbate, and stimulate the most negative aspects of our species."[14]

*"We just want to be connected to something higher.
That could be another person, that could be god,
that could be West Ham United. I think the important
thing is to have the central tenet of your being love,
compassion, and tolerance. Everyone knows that."*

This is almost certainly the most important chapter of this book, as it pertains to reaching unbelieving Millennials with the gospel and equipping Millennials in our churches to carry out Great Commission work. The following explains the general spiritual state of the Millennial generation and what implications that has on ministering to them.

THE RISE OF THE NONES

Before diving into the meat of this chapter studying "spiritual-but-not-religious" Millennials, it is worth taking a bit of time to note the increasing number of Americans who consider themselves "non-religious" or who mark "none" on a survey question which asks about one's religious affiliation.

Perhaps the most comprehensive study of American religiosity in recent years is the Religious Landscape Study conducted by the Pew Research Center. This study surveyed more than 35,000 Americans in 2007 and again in 2014. The two instances of the study allow us to observe how Americans' feelings toward religion changed during that period. All statistics in this chapter are from this study unless indicated otherwise.

The study revealed a lot about American religious beliefs and practices, but perhaps the most fascinating data point was the increasing number of Americans who marked "none" when choosing the religion to which they belong—this has been called by many "The Rise of the Nones."

When Pew released the survey in 2015, I was working for Ed Stetzer, then-Director of LifeWay Research, and we interacted with the data a lot. The prevailing narrative among most media outlets reporting on the Religious Landscape data was, "American Christianity is dying!" In articles we wrote for *Christianity Today*, *CNN*, and *USAToday*, we refuted this narrative. Yes, Americans who have no religious affiliation are increasing in number, but this does not mean Christianity is dying. I concluded our article in *Christianity Today* by saying, "The numerical decline of self-identified American Christianity is more of a purifying bloodletting than it is an arrow to the heart of the church."[15] This is because the Christians who are becoming "nones" were predominately nominal Christians from the Mainline Protestant faith, not evangelicals.

But what about Millennials? No generation has more religiously unaffiliated people than the Millennials. Thirty-six percent of Millennials are religiously unaffiliated, compared to 34 percent of Gen Xers and 23 percent of Baby Boomers.[16] An important caveat here is that as people age, they tend to become more religious. So, as Millennials age, get married, and have children, they are more likely to participate in religious activities, even if they don't necessarily affiliate with a religious group. That means that, while Millennials may be the least religious generation in America today, it may not be true in five or ten years when more of them settle into adulthood. Nevertheless, that more than one-third of Millennials are religiously unaffiliated affects how local churches try to reach them, but we'll explore those implications more in a later chapter. For now, we must continue to another notable Millennial faith phenomenon: the "spiritual but not religious."

SPIRITUAL BUT NOT RELIGIOUS
BY THE NUMBERS

A word of clarity regarding terms in this chapter: one of the age groups identified in the study is "18_29-years-old." When this survey was conducted in 2014, 18_29-year-olds would have been born between 1985 and 1996. This does not give us a full picture of Millennials (born from around 1980 to 1995), but it covers most of them. So, in this chapter, the terms "18_29-year-olds" and "Millennials" will be used interchangeably for the sake of clarity and brevity. Similarly, "30_49-year-olds" will be "Gen Xers," and "50_64-year-olds" will be Baby Boomers. These ranges are not perfectly accurate, but they give a broad view of the realities at play.

According to Pew's 2014 Religious Landscape Study, 73 percent of Millennials believe in God and are either fairly or absolutely certain in this belief. This is lower than any generation to come before them: 83 percent of Gen Xers and 88 percent of Baby Boomers believe this way.

While 73 percent of Millennials say they believe in God with some certainty, only 68 percent of them believe religion is either somewhat or very important, and only 54 percent of them attend religious services more than a few times per year. At the same time, 58 percent of Millennials pray at least once per week, and 69 percent of Millennials report feeling a sense of "spiritual peace and wellbeing" at least once or twice a month. Further, 68 percent of Millennials feel a sense of wonder about the universe at least once or twice per month.

What do all of these statistics actually mean? Compare some of them, and it will become clear.

Almost three-quarters of Millennials believe in "God" with some certainty—not the "God" of any particular faith, just "God" in general. So, while 73 percent of Millennials are certain about the existence of God, only 54 percent of them attend some sort of religious service more than a few times per year. There is roughly a 20 percent disparity between Millennials who believe in "God" and Millennials who attend religious services—this may indicate the level of commitment Millennials have to the God in whom they believe.

They are spiritual, but not religious. After all, only 68 percent of Millennials believe religion is somewhat or very important.

Prayer is a more common religious act among Millennials than attending religious services, which aligns with the common idea that many Millennials are more interested in a strictly personal relationship with "God" than a communal one in a religious setting.

The questions about feeling a sense of "spiritual peace and wellbeing" and "wonder about the universe" are intriguing. Millennials have a sense of wonder about the universe and are at peace about spiritual matters, despite the fact that most of them aren't attending religious services with any regularity.

This tells us that many Millennials believe that something exists beyond, perhaps, what is measurable and physical, and that this existence may be a "God" of some kind. They feel at peace about this reality _ they may even pray to this "God." However, a lower percentage of Millennials are willing to join to a religious institution that gathers together around the worship of a particular "God."

What about the afterlife? How does the afterlife play into the spiritual-but-not-religious mindset of Millennials? Approximately 68 percent of Millennials believe in "heaven," but only 56 percent of them believe in "hell." The difference between those two numbers is fascinating, yet unsurprising. More Millennials believing in a positive version of the afterlife than a negative version aligns with the tendency toward the more common therapeutic use of spirituality, which leads to a necessary discussion on the issue of "moralistic therapeutic deism."

MORALISTIC THERAPEUTIC DEISM: THE COMMON COUNTERFEIT FAITH

Dr. Christian Smith is the William R. Kenan, Jr. Professor of Sociology and Director of the Center for the Study of Religion and Society at the University of Notre Dame. He has written a number of books on the faith of American young people. In his 2005 work *Soul Searching: The Religious and Spiritual Lives of America's Teenagers* he coined the term "Moralistic Therapeutic Deism."

He and his co-author, Melinda Lundquist Denton, write, "We suggest that the de facto dominant religion among contemporary U.S. teenagers is what we might call 'Moralistic Therapeutic Deism.'"[17] The five tenets of Moralistic

Therapeutic Deism are: 1) A God exists who created and orders the world and watches over human life on earth; 2) God wants people to be good, nice, and fair to each other, as taught in the Bible and by most world religions; 3) the central goal in life is to be happy and to feel good about oneself; 4) God does not need to be particularly involved in one's life except when God is needed to resolve a problem; and 5) good people go to heaven when they die.[18]

In August 2016, I had the opportunity to interview Dr. Smith, and I asked him a variety of questions about Millennials and faith. When I asked him what obstacles Moralistic Therapeutic Deism presents for Christian pastors attempting to shepherd a people who hold to it, Dr. Smith said, "The challenge is getting people to see the contrast between Moralistic Therapeutic Deism and real Christianity without being negative, condemning, defensive, sectarian, etc." He says pastors should ask, "Why? And how can they come to see that Christianity is actually vastly superior?"

Indeed, this is a difficult, yet important, question pastors and church leaders must answer. Many American young people, Millennials and Generation Zers both, hold to a faith that believes a "God" is out there, but have little understanding about what that *actually* means. How might pastors, church leaders, parents, and friends engage spiritual-but-not-religious Millennials who may believe in a god that looks very different, yet strangely similar in some ways, to the Christian God?

THREE WAYS TO ENGAGE THE SPIRITUAL-BUT-NOT-RELIGIOUS MILLENNIAL

According to the Religious Landscape Survey, Millennials have not completely abandoned spiritual beliefs or practices. Millennials maintain a sense of spiritual peace and interest in the universe beyond what is seen on earth.

This should lead pastors and church leaders to ask, "How does this affect how I reach out to unbelieving Millennials in my community?" Here are three things to keep in mind.

ENGAGE THE SENSE OF WONDER; DON'T BE AFRAID OF IT.

Millennials feel a sense of wonder about the universe. While they may not be religious, they aren't a bunch of cold-hearted secularists who have no desire to engage with the unseen. Sure, 12 percent of Millennials look to science for guidance on what is right and wrong—which is higher than any other generation _ but that doesn't mean they don't believe something more may lie beyond what science can measure.

As Christians, we can engage the wonder of Millennials and point to the source of that phenomenon: the Creator God of the Bible. Use this wonderment and point people to the starting point and the upholder of it all. Christians have access to the Source of all wonderment in the universe. That Millennials are captivated by a sense of wonder must be seen as an evangelistic *advantage* not as an *obstacle*. Tap into this wonder and direct it toward the Source.

PROBE FOR THE SOURCE OF "SPIRITUAL PEACE."

Why do Millennials have such a sense of spiritual peace? Is it because they truly believe God exists and has their best interests at heart? Only 51 percent of Millennials believe the Bible is the Word of God, so how do they form any ideas about God that would give them any sense of spiritual peace? These are not *theoretical* questions—Christians must learn what the Millennials in our churches and communities think and have conversations that lead them to find peace in the personal God of the Bible rather than an impersonal, unknown deity far beyond the universe that (hopefully) wants what is best for the people of earth.

We have to understand that many of the non-Christian, spiritual-but-not-religious Millennials in our communities are likely content with where they stand spiritually. Christians should talk with them, ask questions, and identify the source of this "spiritual peace," then figure out how it may fall short of the gospel and graciously make that clear.

PROVIDE A BETTER WAY.

Finally, when we engage the sense of wonder and spiritual peace among Millennials, we must provide a better way—the only Way, the gospel of Jesus. Paul writes in Romans 1:16, "For I am not ashamed of the gospel, because it is the power of God for salvation to everyone who believes, first to the Jew, and also to the Greek." And also to the Millennial who is spiritual-but-not-religious. In our attempts to reach unbelieving Millennials with the gospel of Jesus, number crunching and analysis is not going to save anyone. The gospel *alone* is the power of God for salvation to everyone who believes. We can learn as much about Millennials' spiritual preferences as we can contain in our brains, but if we don't share the gospel with them, we've wasted our time.

The research shows these young people are not hard-and-fast naturalists who only believe in what they can see in front of their faces. They ponder the spiritual. They wonder about the universe. Engage these feelings and point them to their ultimate, eternal fulfillment. Millennials have feelings of spiritual wonder and faith for a *reason*. This is not a coincidence. We are all made to worship and engage in the spiritual wonderment of the glory of God. This longing, this feeling of something beyond, is only natural. It is a thirst that can only be satisfied by the gospel of Jesus Christ. But because of past experiences or hardness of heart, many Millennials will resist the Christian gospel as the fulfillment of their spiritual longings. The gospel can triumph over this obstacle.

Young people may be open to the things of Jesus no matter how closed they may be to the local church. Personal, intentional relationships and living on mission in everyday life have never been so important. I know that, over the decades, battles have been fought among various sects of evangelicalism about the "best way" to do evangelism. However we share the gospel with Millennials, we need to just *do it*. I will say, however, that because of what we know about Millennials and how they view faith and religion, relational methods of evangelism may be more effective at reaching this generation than ever before. An "evangelistic encounter" with a Millennial in our communities may look more like a six-month relationship than a six-minute conversation about life after death in a grocery store checkout line.

We must show and share Jesus in our homes, workplaces, and wherever else we may be. Millennials may stay away from church, but that doesn't mean they aren't wondering what goes on in there.

INTERESTED BUT WARY

A significant portion of Millennials do not affiliate with a religious group but do consider themselves interested in spiritual matters. At first glance this reality may seem discouraging, but it could be worse. If Millennials considered themselves both not religious *and* not spiritual, reaching them could be much more difficult. They would be repulsed by any conversation about faith. However, because Millennials are at least interested in spiritual matters, even if they avoid "religion," the door is open to have spiritual conversations with them, perhaps most appropriately in a non-religious setting like a coffee shop or otherwise. They are interested, but because of past experiences with churches or other religious institutions, they are wary.

We've covered a lot in this chapter, and like I said at the beginning, I think it is perhaps the most important, most valuable chapter in the whole book. The next section focuses on applying what we've learned in this chapter to reaching unbelieving Millennials.

4/   **BE TRUSTWORTHY**

In November of 2008, the fall of my senior year of high school, I decided to attend Taylor University in Upland, Indiana, conditional upon getting enough in scholarship money to lower the cost equal to that of a state school. Our family was upper-middle class, so attending a private Christian liberal arts school was not out of the question. But to avoid massive student loans, I was going to need a significant amount of scholarship help.

In January of 2009, two months after I committed to a very expensive private university and five months before I graduated high school, my dad lost his job of 27 years at IBM. The company was cutting jobs in order to stay afloat amidst the Great Recession of 2008.

This was an incredibly difficult time for my family, particularly my dad. When he graduated from Purdue University in the early 1980s, he walked straight into a job with IBM. It was the only job he had ever known. The majority of his time there, he was able to work from home, and my mom didn't have to work. I was blessed with two parents who were *always* home to pick me up from school, help me with my homework, and coach my baseball teams. Dad losing his job was also hard on me. When I decided to attend Taylor, I already felt a little guilty because of how much it cost, but when my dad lost his job, I felt like the most selfish person in the world. My dad didn't have a job, and I was expecting my parents to pay for private school because I certainly wasn't going to be able to pay for it.

My dad found another job and I was able to attend Taylor, but those months changed me. I became skeptical of banks and the government. I intended to major in English Education, and I knew high school English teacher positions would be available to me (if I could actually afford school, that is), but I wasn't sure who to trust with the little money I had. Gas prices continued to skyrocket, which I thought was because companies wanted to take advantage of us amidst dire economic times. I developed a deep cynicism toward institutions bureaucratic, banking, and otherwise.

This experience is not unique to me. The Great Recession almost certainly affected all Millennials in one way or another, if not with job loss, then with something else. For Millennials like me, this was just one of the many world events that shrank our trust in institutions that surround us. This is not to say Gen Xers or Baby Boomers had it easy_ they had their tragedies too—but a few events that took place in the developmental years of many Millennials radically shaped how they think about institutions.

INSTITUTIONAL MISTRUST BY THE NUMBERS

One of the best-known attributes of the Millennial generation is their distrust of institutions. Whenever I read an article about Millennials in the workplace or Millennials in the church, one of the first things the article says is, "Millennials don't trust institutions." This is true_ Millennials are more detached from institutions like the government and the church than any generation of Americans to come before them—but to what extent?

Pew's *Millennials in Adulthood* study provides data toward this end. A full 50 percent of Millennials consider themselves political independents, compared to just 39 percent of Gen Xers and 37 percent of Baby Boomers. Likewise, 29 percent of Millennials identify as religiously unaffiliated, compared to just 21 percent of Gen Xers and 16 percent of Baby Boomers.[19]

A 2015 Harvard Youth Poll gathered data that concurs with Pew regarding Millennial distrust of government institutions. Approximately 49 percent of Millennials have "not much" (35 percent or "no" (14 percent confidence in the fairness of the United States justice system, and the same percentage of Millennials said they had "some" or "a lot" of confidence in the justice system[20]—in case we needed any more evidence that the country is divided on such matters. Also, most of these statistics refer to institutional distrust, but it should also be noted that only 19 percent of Millennials believe that most people, generally speaking, can be trusted.[21]

I could bore readers with statistics all day, but these statistics represent actual events that changed how Millennials think about the world, much like the personal experience I explained above. What happened to erode the institutional trust of Millennials?

THE WORLD THAT STOLE OUR TRUST

Millennials have a lack of institutional trust_it's an epidemic. But why? What has caused Millennials to distrust the great institutions of society like governments, churches, and banks? Systemic institutional distrust happens because of a million paper cuts rather than because of a few major issues. But to say that Millennials' distrust of institutions is divorced from major world events would be foolish. What are the roots of Millennial distrust of institutions? Here are a few major events that may have had some effect.

THE (OTHER) DATE THAT WILL LIVE IN INFAMY: SEPTEMBER 11, 2001

On September 11, 2001, I was 10 years old, in the fifth grade, and getting ready for school. The television in our kitchen was regularly tuned to ABC's *Good Morning America* as we ate breakfast and packed lunches. I was standing at the bar in our kitchen when Charlie Gibson and Diane Sawyer broke news that a plane had crashed into one of the World Trade Center buildings in New York City. "Mom," I said, "Someone accidentally crashed a plane into a building in New York City." I walked out of the room for a few minutes, and by the time I had come back, it had happened again. "Mom, a second plane accidentally hit the other one," I said. "Oh honey," she replied, "I don't think that's an accident." At age 10, it simply did not register that someone would do such a thing intentionally.

That day I learned that the United States was not untouchable, and the subsequent months and years of war would teach me that we weren't perfect, either. On September 11, 2001, Millennials ranged in age from 21 to one. Because of this, the tragic events of that day affected Millennials in different ways, but many of them lost faith in the government and its ability to keep us safe.

THE SEXUAL ABUSE TRAGEDY IN THE CATHOLIC CHURCH

Approximately 16 percent of Millennials self-identify as Roman Catholic. Other generations have much higher shares of Catholic representation: 23 percent of Baby Boomers are Catholic, and 21 percent of Gen Xers are Catholic.[22] Many Millennials, particularly older Millennials born between 1981 and 1989 would have been old enough to remember the tragic revelation of sexual abuse in the Roman Catholic Church that broke wide open in the early 2000s.

After the *Boston Globe* broke open the story about sexual abuse in the Boston archdiocese, more and more allegations and stories surfaced about sexual abuse within the Catholic Church throughout the United States and Ireland. The reality of the abuse was so grotesque and widespread that the matter eventually reached the Vatican and led to serious repercussions legally and otherwise.

For many young people, the sexual abuse tragedy in the Catholic Church simply confirmed that churches cannot be trusted. Most young Millennials would have been too young to know exactly what was going on, but older Millennials would have been old enough to hear about the abuse and lose trust in their local church, whether they were Catholic or not.

THE GREAT RECESSION

According to the U. S. Bureau of Labor Statistics, in November 2007 the unemployment rate in the United States was 4.7 percent. In October 2009, the unemployment rate was 10 percent. According to the U.S. Department of Labor, almost nine million jobs were eliminated between February 2008 and February 2010. I told my Great Recession story at the beginning of this chapter, and our family was quite fortunate. My dad was able to find a new job within a month or two, which was a blessing even if the new job wasn't ideal.

Families around the country had to find ways to make ends meet, and this was all in the midst of many Millennials' most important developmental periods. Older Millennials were already in the workforce, but many Millennials were either in high school or in college and preparing to start their careers . . . or so they hoped. The economic outlook was bleak, and while September 11 may have eroded Millennials' trust in the government to protect them from harm, the Great Recession led many Millennials to distrust the economic stability of the United States.

THREE REASONS HONESTY IS THE BEST POLICY FOR REACHING MILLENNIALS

First, honesty fosters openness. My wife and I are blessed to be members at a local church that models this as well as I have ever seen. Our church's mission is to "Multiply gospel change for broken people on purpose." The mission statement is intentional because the Lord has, for some reason, seen fit to fill our church with story after story of brokenness. The old phrase, "It's okay to not be okay," is cheesy and sometimes wrongly used to ignore sin, but I think it is valuable if understood rightly. A local church that hopes to reach Millennials must not create a culture that makes it seem like everyone is "Doing great!" all the time. A local church that hopes to reach Millennials must create a culture in which it is okay to share how sin has broken the lives of the people without fear of gossip or other such repercussions, all with the understanding that we must put aside brokenness in our pursuit of Christlikeness.

Second, honesty welcomes involvement. If your church has a sort of secret group within the church that actually makes all of the decisions _a sort of unofficial leadership team that pulls all the levers _ this is going to make it difficult for a Millennial to join your church and get involved. When we lead our churches in a way that communicates openness and honesty, an unbelieving Millennial who darkens the door of a local church may be more willing to get involved and learn more about what it means to be a part of a local church and trust in Jesus. We should be as upfront as we can about the decisions we make in the church, such as what the offering money is being used for and what our overall mission is. The more honest and open we are with our churches, the more likely an unbelieving Millennial is going to be to stick around and learn more about what's going on.

Third, honesty is biblical. The value of honesty is on display throughout the Scriptures. It made the stone tablets, as it is written in Exodus 20:16, "Do not give false testimony against your neighbor." Proverbs 19:1 says, "Better a poor person who lives with integrity than someone who has deceitful lips and is a fool." Paul writes in Colossians 3:9 that it is part of the old self, and he writes in Ephesians 4:25 that, being members of one another, we are to "put away lying." Christians are honest with each other. This does not mean Christians are to go out of their way telling everyone what's on their minds at all times, but it does mean that we cannot lie or deceive in hopes of benefitting ourselves, hiding sin, or for some other nefarious purpose. Honesty is biblical, and the Scriptures are clear that those who are honest avoid the perils of those who deceive. Pastors and church leaders who put a façade will struggle to reach Millennials for a number of reasons, the foremost of which is that it is unbiblical.

So, honesty is important, but how does a ministry practically maintain a culture of honesty? What does that look like, and what steps can be taken to establish such an environment?

THREE WAYS TO MAINTAIN A TRUSTWORTHY MINISTRY

First, model humility. The next chapter is entirely devoted to the importance of humility, but it is important to mention here as a means of maintaining a culture of honesty. Too often, passionate Christians (including pastors and church leaders) take to social media and other forms of communication to defend a doctrine or political stance without taking into consideration the importance of humility. Social media has made it too easy for us to justify blasting people who think differently than us, and many Christians attack the sins of others without considering the pride in their own hearts.

Humility is attractive. Pride is disgusting. Humility is Christ-like. Pride is sinful.

It's hard to trust someone who is so prideful he or she cannot see his own faults. A church that models humility is more likely to win the trust of unbelieving Millennials because it tells them, "We know we're sinners even though Jesus has saved us, and that means we're no better than you." One of the most common complaints about church people is, "They think they're better than everyone else." Sometimes this is an unfair representation, but sometimes it's not_Christians turn their noses up at people, too. It is important that our churches create a culture in which such self-righteousness is unwelcome and uncomfortable.

Humility can be tough, especially when our own sin and foolishness makes itself blatantly apparent. We ought to take a moment to think of who we are in light of who God is, and perhaps we'll treat others as no better than ourselves.

Second, avoid hypocrisy. I know, I know, it's not really *possible* to avoid hypocrisy. Being a hypocrite is a basic effect of sin—all of us are hypocrites at some point or another. Truthfully, the Christian life is *defined* by hypocrisy. We say, "It is important to be like Christ," and we routinely show ourselves and those around us that we are not yet like Christ. What is most important, perhaps, rather than achieving a life free of hypocrisy, is being willing to acknowledge and own our hypocrisy. A Christian who denies his or her hypocrisy is either ignorant or dishonest. Recognizing and dealing with the log in our own eyes before going after an unbelieving Millennial about his or her sin is vital in the effort to reach young people with the gospel.

For instance, if you were to get dinner with a new, unbelieving Millennial in your church and you started to address their sin without somehow acknowledging your own, you're unlikely to get another chance to share the gospel with them. *You* know you're a sinner, but the unbelieving Millennials you want to reach may not know that you're self-aware enough to recognize your own sin. Being upfront and honest about our own shortcomings before we call out the sins of an unbelieving young person is helpful as we seek to share the gospel.

Third, don't sugarcoat. Sugarcoating truth is ultimately untruth and blatant dishonesty. The temptation to sugarcoat difficult truths of the Scripture is strong, especially when attempting to minister to a generation of people that seem to be straying from the faith of their parents in many ways. Sugarcoating truth is deceiving. Sure, preaching a text about the wrath of God with a spoonful of sugar may help us attract Millennials initially, but it likely won't keep them around in the long run. Sooner or later, as the young people in our churches mature in their faith, they're going to realize that the Bible isn't as full of butterflies and rainbows as they once thought it was. This realization can ultimately lead to not only a distrust of the pastor but also a distrust of the God they thought they knew. We must be honest with our churches and the young people in them. Honestly proclaiming the difficult truths of the Bible goes a long way in building trust with Millennials. We must not try to sell a product from the pulpit. Proclaim Jesus and the gospel_difficult truths and all.

TRUST IS EARNED, NOT GIVEN

Millennials simply don't trust a lot of the same people and institutions their parents and grandparents did. The internet plays a significant role in this. Millennials are able to research a claim made by an authority figure in seconds_an impossibility for generations who came before.

Whereas Baby Boomers may have looked at churches or certain government agencies with a bit of confidence,

Millennials often only see vulnerability and uncertainty. Pastors and church leaders: we have been tasked with reaching unbelieving Millennials because Millennials are included in the Great Commission as much as anyone else. If we hope to reach Millennials, we must be honest with them. Ministry defined by a lack of transparency among hypocritical leaders who sugarcoat the truths of the gospel will not create an opportunity to share the gospel with Millennials no matter how dynamic the worship or how delicious the church coffee.

In order for pastors and church leaders to reach unbelieving Millennials effectively, there must be a culture of honesty and transparency that acknowledges brokenness and sin and points to ultimate hope in the gospel. A façade of success and perfection may attract a Baby Boomer businessman who wants his church to run as smoothly as his corporation, but it will not attract an unbelieving Millennial who understands that not everything is perfect and pristine. Want to reach a generation of people who distrust institutions? Take intentional steps to be trustworthy. Understand that trust will have to be earned; it will not be given.

5/   **BE HUMBLE**

I was a real jerk in high school. I went to church and was very active in my youth group, but the sanctifying work of the Holy Spirit seemed to be lagging behind my salvation a bit. I have never had a problem speaking my mind, and back in high school—and on my weak days, even now—I operated with the all-too-common attitude that, "If you're offended by the truth I speak, that's your problem, not mine. Get over it."

What high school Chris did not yet understand, and what current me too often forgets, is that speaking the truth is not license to be offensive in tone, body language, or otherwise. Ultimately, this brashness was rooted in an abundance of sinful pride, with which I still struggle today.

My high school youth pastor, Phil Knuth, has been one of the most formative theological forces in my life. One of the most effective attributes of Phil's ministry was his ability to simply define common Christian words that we often use without fully understanding. You know the words: "grace," "mercy," "love," and others. Phil gave legs to the Christian words that often feel empty because they're tossed around recklessly. One of the words he defined for us was "humility." As someone who was a prideful high school student, it was important for me to understand what humility meant because it was virtually absent from my life. "Humility," Phil taught us, "is knowing who *we are* in light of who *God is*." That single definition, which is only one of many ways "humility" could be explained, changed my life. I no longer thought humility was this sort of self-hate, as it is sometimes wrongly characterized. Humility is simply having a right understanding of who *we are* in light of who *God is*.

If we hope to reach unbelieving Millennials in our communities, we must approach them humbly. Riding into the lives of unbelieving Millennials on a spiritual high horse smells bad . . . for multiple reasons. Effectively reaching unbelieving Millennials with the gospel requires us to present ourselves as people who still need the gospel we're offering, not as those who has already accomplished it.

But, what is the biblical basis for humility and the abolition of pride in the heart of God's people?

THE NECESSITY OF HUMILITY

We have earned nothing but separation from God, and yet we conduct our lives as though we are our own gods. In our sin, we have attempted to exchange our rule over all creation for ruling over all that is true, having the authority to decide what is and what isn't true. We are plagued by a false understanding of who we are in light of who God is. We have exchanged the truth that we are *like* God for the lie that we *are* gods. In short, we have a pride problem. God, knowing us better than we know ourselves, makes clear the necessity of humility in his Word. In the Old Testament humility is often seen through a vertical lens, in regard to one's relationship with God. In the New Testament humility is more frequently seen through a horizontal lens, in regard to one's relationship with others.

HUMILITY AND DEPENDENCE ON GOD

Andrew Murray writes in his classic, little book *Humility*, "Humility, the place of entire dependence on God, is, from the very nature of things, the first duty and the highest virtue of the creature, and the root of every virtue."[23] Indeed, the Scriptures attest to this truth.

One of the earliest clear examples of humility comes from Abraham's relationship with God. Abraham is one of the few characters in the Old Testament who interacts with God as friend, and yet, when he comes before God on behalf of Sodom—begging God to spare the righteous who inhabit the city from his impending expression of wrath—Abraham calls himself "dust and ashes" before God (Gen 18:27). In this moment Abraham is completely dependent upon God for the salvation of the righteous in Sodom; he is powerless. In this moment Abraham knows who he is in light of who God is: dust and ashes.

In Psalm 22_the first verse of which Jesus Christ quotes on the cross in his dying moments—David writes a desperate lament, crying out for God in his desperation. David writes in verse 26, "The humble will eat and be satisfied; those who seek the Lord will praise him." Amidst David's desperate lament: there is hope: God will remember and satisfy the humble. Psalm 149:4 says the Lord "adorns the humble with salvation."

Humility and a dependence upon God go hand in hand. Pastors and church leaders who lead with a spirit of pride do not reach unbelieving Millennials with the gospel because prideful pastors and church leaders do not depend on the Lord to reach unbelieving Millennials with the gospel. In sinful pride, they believe that with the right music and blend of coffee they can reach multitudes of Millennials. This is not the case.

In Zechariah 9:9, salvation for Zion comes humbly mounted on a donkey. Christ is the epitome of humility and the ultimate refuge for a dependence on God. Murray writes, "Christ is the humility of God embodied in human nature."[24] Philippians 2:8 says that Christ, after emptying himself, "humbled himself by becoming obedient to the point of death—even to death on a cross." Jesus Christ, the Son of God, when he came to die knew who he is in light of who his Father is: he is the obedient, sinless Son sent to die on behalf of the prideful, rebellious people. Even the Son of God humbled himself to utter dependence on the Father. If he did, how can we not?

HUMILITY AND LOVE FOR OTHERS

Many New Testament passages mentioning humility deal with humbling oneself before others rather than before God in worship or otherwise. A number of New Testament passages about humility have a *horizontal* emphasis rather than a more *vertical* emphasis. What follows are a few key New Testament passages that highlight the connection between humility and loving others.

First, in Mark 9:35 Jesus says to the twelve disciples, "If anyone wants to be first, he must be last and servant of all." This saying of Jesus comes in the context of the disciples discussing who is greatest among them. In verse 34 Mark writes that when Jesus asked what they were talking about, they kept silent_they were ashamed. The disciples didn't want to answer Jesus because they knew that arguing about who among them was greatest was not compatible with Jesus and what he had been teaching them. Before God, one cannot be great if one does not consider others before himself. Murray writes in *Humility*, "Humility before God is nothing if not proved in humility before men."[25]

Second, in John 13:14_15 Jesus says to his disciples at the Last Supper, "So if I, your Lord and Teacher, have washed your feet, you also ought to wash one another's feet. For I have given you an example, that you also should do just as I have done for you." Jesus washing the disciples' feet at the Last Supper is not meant to be a prescription for Christian teachers to literally wash the feet of their disciples. Rather, when Jesus washes his disciples' feet, he is showing them (and us) that God in the flesh is not too important to serve those whom he leads. And, if God in the flesh is not too important to serve those whom he leads, neither are pastors and other church leaders, or any follower of Christ. Despite being the Son of God, Jesus humbly loves those who follow him. If any human in history should have license to be proud of himself, it would be Jesus; but he knows that humility is greater than pride.

Third, Paul writes in Philippians 2:3, "Do nothing out of selfish ambition or conceit, but in humility consider others as more important than yourselves." Later, he exhorts his readers to look out for the interests of others, adopting the same attitude as Christ. The temptation to pursue our own selfish agendas will be strong as long as we are sinners, but for the sake of the church and because we desire to be more like Christ, we must pursue others' needs before our own wants. We must, by the power of the Holy Spirit, consider others as more important than ourselves. We must do this not to be saved but to live out the salvation we've been given in the gospel.

Humility is *difficult*, and though it may not be listed as a "fruit of the Spirit" in Galatians 5, it is a fruit of a life defined by the selfless love of Christ. As people who claim to be transformed by the gospel, humility must increasingly color how we relate to God and to others. We must pursue humility so that we might show others the glorious work of the Holy Spirit in the lives of people who were once defined by their brokenness but are now defined by how the gospel makes them whole.

THE FRUIT OF HUMILITY

This is a book about reaching Millennials, not a book about humility, so we must answer the question, Why does humility matter for reaching unbelieving Millennials with the gospel?

First, humility fosters trust, the importance of which was outlined in the previous chapter. Christians, especially pastors and church leaders, must understand that many unbelieving Millennials see Christians as just a bunch of hypocrites: people who say they care about morality but don't act like it. Is this stereotype unfair? Maybe, but non-Christians see Christians this way whether we like it or not. Because many unbelieving Millennials are going to view Christians with a bit of skepticism, our ministry to unbelieving, skeptical Millennials will start with breaking down walls before any sort of real relationship can be built. One way Christians break down walls with unbelieving Millennials is by being humble.

For example, if a pastor is talking to an unbelieving Millennial about the origins of the earth, and the unbelieving Millennial cites a scientific theory with which the pastor is unfamiliar, what should the pastor do? Too often, the pastor's inclination is to dismiss the skeptic's point or to pretend like he is well versed in scientific matters. Instead, the pastor may want to consider humbly saying to the skeptic, "I'm really not sure how that theory jives with Christian views on this subject. Can I do some research and get back to you?" Here the pastor humbly admits that he's out of his depth and needs to come back after some research.

For another example, one of the best ways to address the common Millennial claim that "Christians are hypocrites," is to just *own* it. I believe that, when it comes to having conversations with unbelievers, Christians cannot acknowledge their own sin and need for a Savior enough. I have never heard an unbeliever say, "Man, those Christians are just too aware of how messed up they are." No! The most common complaint I have heard from unbelieving Millennials about Christians is that they act like they are *perfect* because they are perceived as always calling out the sins of *others* and never paying adequate attention to their *own*.

For instance, when we have conversations with family members or neighbors who are not believers, we should acknowledge that we see ourselves as sinners just like we see others as sinners. This humility fosters trust because it says, "I know that I am not exempt from the need for the gospel I am presenting to this person." It is off-putting when

Christians talk like people who believe they never needed the gospel instead of people who have been saved by the gospel. Acknowledging this reality as we talk with unbelieving Millennials (or anyone else) can help foster trust because it shows them we are aware we are not exceptional—we are broken and in need just like them.

Second, humility fosters sacrificial love. As was made clear in Jesus's washing of the disciples' feet, when we humble ourselves, our humility leads us to love others sacrificially. It is easy to love others in ways that are comfortable for us, but it is difficult to love others in ways that make us uncomfortable. When we think highly of ourselves, it is difficult to see the value in putting others first. But, when we rightly see how lowly we are in light of who God is, it is easier to hold others in higher regard than we hold ourselves.

How does this apply to humbly reaching unbelieving Millennials? A lot of unbelieving Millennials in our communities simply need to be loved in a way that does not leave them broken and abandoned. Millennials grew up in a culture in which nearly 50 percent of marriages ended in divorce, which means many of them have an intimate understanding of what selfish love looks like, but may have no idea what sacrificial love looks like.[26] If Christians reach out to unbelieving Millennials in their communities in humility with the hope of building trust and relationship, the body of

Christ will have the opportunity to show the love of Christ to unbelieving Millennials. In John 13:35 Jesus says, "By this everyone will know that you are my disciples, if you love one another." Indeed, even beyond that, perhaps one of the most direct ways an unbeliever can come to know the sacrificial love of Jesus is by being sacrificially loved by his followers. If we want to reach unbelieving Millennials in our communities, we must show them the selfless love that Christ has shown us. Humble love says, "Your needs are more important than my needs, and if our relationship ever ends, I want to leave you better off than I found you."

Third, humility fosters genuine community. As you consider the unbelieving Millennials in your community and how you might reach out to them, consider their need for community. As of 2017, Millennials are somewhere between 20 and 37 years old. This time of life can be lonely for any generation, but especially Millennials. According to Pew's *Millennials in Adulthood* research, just 26 percent of Millennials are married at ages 18 to 32, compared to 36 percent of Gen Xers and 48 percent of Baby Boomers when they were between those ages. Speaking from recent experience, even as a married Millennial the first five years after college can be incredibly lonely, especially living far from family like my wife and I are. Praise God we have the local church that has blessed us with a community that loves us and that we love, but some unbelieving Millennials often struggle to find community after college because they are not part of a local church and many remain unmarried.

Christians can reach unbelieving Millennials in their communities by providing a genuine community found nowhere else, one characterized by a humility that can only be found in those who have been transformed by the gospel. Christians alone have access to true humility. Why? Because only Christians can say, "I know I deserve eternal separation from God because of my sin, and it is only because of the life, death, and resurrection of Jesus that I am able to draw my next breath, let alone spend eternity in glory." One who does not trust in God cannot truly understand who he is in light of who God is.

Because only Christians understand humility in its purest sense, only Christians can provide a community of people who are able to be completely and utterly vulnerable with one another before God. This sort of community is refreshing and transformative even for a Millennial who is not yet sure about Jesus and the gospel. The idea that a community of people can gather together, share their mistakes, their triumphs, their scars, their fears, and their joys without abandoning one another is truly attractive even before it is made clear that this is because of Christ and what he has done on behalf of that community of people. This is why I think the groups ministry in the local church is the single greatest outreach tool when it comes to reaching unbelieving Millennials. However, such a community cannot exist without the humility the Holy Spirit gives us when we understand that we are fully dependent on God for both the next breath and the next life. This is not to say Christian community is perfect, but it can reach a depth of love and understanding that no other community can.

HUMILITY IS THE KEY TO COMMUNITY

Humility is knowing who we are in light of who God is. Scripture is clear: humility has both *vertical* and *horizontal* implications. Whether or not we know who we are in light of who God is will affect our relationship with God and our relationships with others. If we do not rightly understand who we are in relation to God, we will refuse to worship him or worship him wrongly. Further, if we do not understand who we are in relation to God, we will be unable to love others as greater than ourselves as Christ has loved us. Humility is vital to reaching unbelieving Millennials with the gospel because it uniquely fosters trust, love, and community \. By humbly building trust with unbelieving Millennials, you will gain opportunities to love them sacrificially and involve them in a community the likes of which can be found nowhere else.

6/ **BE CLEAR**

When I was in high school I earned the worst grade of my life: a C-. For some that grade is appalling; for others it is probably acceptable. In most cases it would have been unacceptable in my home growing up, but for this particular class it was just fine. It was my sophomore math class: honors advanced algebra. I was a straight-A student in every class in high school except two of my math classes, and it wasn't for lack of knowledge as much as it was for lack of *caring*. My dad and I would sit at the kitchen table hovering over equations for hours after dinner, and I would say, sometimes through tears, "I DON'T KNOW WHY THIS MATTERS AND I AM DONE CARING!" Ultimately, the reason I got a C- in sophomore math was because I didn't know *why* it mattered to learn it, and my teacher wouldn't tell me when I asked her. I struggle to do anything without knowing precisely why I am doing it, and I am not alone—this is a common Millennial trait.

Answering the question "Why?" is vital to communicating with clarity. I am a stickler about clear communication, even to the point of being annoying. Words matter, and it bothers me when people throw them around haphazardly. Christians have a responsibility to communicate the truths of the Christian faith with clarity. If we are going to reach unbelieving Millennials, we must communicate with clarity, and we will *not* be able to avoid the question "Why?"

WE MUST HAVE AN ANSWER FOR THE QUESTION "WHY?"

Simon Sinek, a renowned leadership consultant, is famously known for his book *Start with Why* and the viral TED talk built upon this concept. In the book and the TED talk, Sinek makes the point that, "People don't buy *what* you do; they buy *why* you do it."[27] The same, in a sense, could be applied to the local church and how it distinguishes itself from other religions. Some aspects of the "what" of Christianity are obedience and love and eternity and worship—many faiths offer such things. Many of the facets of Christianity are not unique to Christianity. However, the "why" of Christianity is the gospel of Jesus Christ—it is the fuel for any and all obedience, love, worship, and hope of eternity in the life of the Christian. This is what sets Christianity apart _ no other faith has the "why" that Christianity has. In no other system of faith did God die for his people in order that they might be saved. Unbelieving Millennials are not likely to buy into *what* Christians do—they are more likely to buy into *why* we do it.

A common misconception persists about why young people, specifically Millennials, ask the question "Why?" In past generations, asking the question "Why?" communicated disrespect or distrust. Today that mindset often leads to unhelpful attempts at conversation because the person who has been asked "Why?" often feels defensive and unable to answer the question.

It is important to acknowledge here that Millennials asking the question "Why?" are often doing so with no disrespect or malicious intent. Millennials are natives to the digital age. They have grown up having to sift through facts and fiction on the internet as they research for school projects or settle an argument on social media.

Millennials, because of their vast exposure to information and misinformation, are perhaps more likely to be skeptical than their parents or grandparents were. This dominant factor that leads Millennials to ask "Why?" more than previous generations. If pastors and church leaders react defensively to an unbelieving Millennial asking "Why?" about a theological concept, the conversation will be hindered and may not advance beyond this point.

Have a posture of humility and be willing to meet people where they are. Figure out why they're asking "Why?," what their needs are, and how the gospel addresses those needs.

THREE STEPS TO COMMUNICATE MORE EFFECTIVELY

Clear, effective communication is vital in any ministry context, but it is especially important to connecting with people of cultural, racial, or other backgrounds that may be different from our own. A single miscommunication, or a pattern of miscommunication, can devastate our attempts to share the gospel with unbelievers who communicate differently than we do. Pastors and church leaders who reach out to unbelievers bear the responsibility to communicate in the context of the unbelievers, not vice versa. But how might pastors and church leaders communicate more effectively with Millennials specifically? I offer three steps.

First, shut our mouths and open our ears. Pastors and church leaders, as we work to reach out to unbelieving Millennials in our communities, we must understand the importance of listening to their feelings, pain, doubts, anger, and other potentially unsavory thoughts. Few Millennials grew up in homes or communities in which faith was completely non-existent. So we must understand that there may be barriers to faith that we have to knock down before any foundations of faith can be established.

Listening to Millennials describe poor experiences they have had with Christian churches or other organized religions may be difficult. Their reasoning may be rife with anecdotal experiences masked as gross generalizations. That does not give us license to stop listening. In order to effectively engaging them, they must know that we *care* about them as people, not just as souls to be saved. And the easiest way to do that is to remain silent rather than speaking up whenever we want.

Listening before we speak not only communicates that we care, but it's practical, too. If we hope to share the gospel with an unbelieving Millennial in over coffee, we would be wise to listen to their story first. Identifying their values and hearing their doubts may allow us to tailor a gospel presentation to who they are. If we launch into the gospel presentation without taking into consideration his/her personal narrative, we haven't shown that we care about him/her. Of course, the gospel is the power of God to save, so of it can overcome our poor communication, but that doesn't give mean we can be sloppy communicators. We should listen before we speak as we try to reach unbelieving Millennials.

Second, effective communication requires us to give others the benefit of the doubt. We will better communicate better with Millennials if we take them at their word, giving them the benefit of the doubt about what they say and believe. Millennials are skeptical about matters of faith, and it is also understandable that people of faith may be a bit skeptical of Millennials' worldviews too. However, as we try to reach Millennials with the gospel, we would be wise to assume the best of their motives and intentions, and converse on their "home field." This can be a confusing concept, so let me give an example.

Earlier I mentioned my unbelieving Millennial friend, Kurt. I have periodic conversations about life, politics, and faith with him online. Kurt considers himself spiritual but not religious and tends to live by a "love everybody, live-and-let-live" sort of ethic. When Kurt and I talk about issues such as the relationship of science and faith or what makes Christianity different from other religions, we have significant disagreements, but we are able to have long, civil discussions *online*, of all places. A big reason for this is because we give each other the benefit of the doubt. We know that, as we ask questions of each other, we are not looking to insult each other's intelligence or question each other's character. We have a mutual respect for one another. We assume the best about one another.

This is vital in our attempts to reach unbelieving Millennials. This is not about avoiding hurt feelings; this is about not adding unnecessary offense to an already offensive gospel. This is about doing our part to establish and maintain a mutual respect that will undergird and enhance our conversations moving forward. As we converse with unbelieving Millennials who have vastly different worldviews than us, it is wise to remember, "No matter how wrong I know this person is, he or she is simply looking for truth to live the best life he or she can." When we talk with a Millennial who has a worldview different from our own, we need to recognize that they have the same goal we do: to live faithful to the truth of the world. They simply misunderstand that truth, and we have the opportunity to humbly present it to them in love.

Third, effective communication requires us to speak as we would like to be spoken to. This is the Golden Rule of communication, and I believe its importance is pretty self-explanatory. Unfortunately, in the age of the social internet, this principle has been widely disregarded by Christians and non-Christians alike. I should be clear: the internet is not at fault for this phenomenon. We are. The internet has simply been a tool to enable our sinful hearts to communicate with a lack of love, charity, and respect. Facebook and YouTube comment sections are where the Golden Rule of communication goes to die, but I am concerned that this virtual reality is seeping into our physical reality.

As we work to reach unbelieving Millennials in our communities with the gospel, it is important that we communicate with them with the same compassion and respect that we expect to receive when others engage us. A Millennial is no less deserving of compassion and respect because he or she does not believe the gospel or lives a life contrary to the Scriptures. Our efforts to reach them will be enhanced, not undermined, by communicating with love that makes our conversation feel encouraging even if the person does not come to trust Christ or believe the same way we do.

WATCHING OUR SPEECH

Paul writes in Colossians 4:5_6, "Act wisely toward outsiders, making the most of the time. Let our speech always be gracious, seasoned with salt, so that you may know how you should answer each person." As we engage with Millennials who are "outsiders" because they do not trust Jesus for salvation, we must make the most of our time. We do this by letting our speech be characterized by grace, seasoned with the salt of the truth, so that we might engage in wisdom and love.

We cannot become defensive when Millennials ask "Why?" In order to engage effectively, we must communicate by listening, giving the other the benefit of the doubt, and following the Golden Rule of Communication: communicating as we would like to others to communicate with us.

SECTION

THREE

EQUIPPING

7/ **LEARN TOGETHER**

C hurch frustrated me when I was in elementary school. I remember my pastor taking time at the end of almost every church service to talk about "asking Jesus into your heart" and "being saved from your sin." I remember thinking in my young mind, "Well, I don't know if this Christian thing is real, but it would probably be smart to cover my bases and ask Jesus into my heart just in case." I also remember feeling sort of left out because I hadn't asked Jesus into my heart yet. I was frustrated because he kept talking about "asking Jesus into your heart" like it was the most important thing in the world, but I didn't really know how to do it. How do you ask an invisible person who lived a long time ago to occupy the organ in your chest that pumps blood to your body?

Finally, one Sunday morning in my fourth-grade Sunday school class, I prayed "the sinner's prayer," and nothing about my life changed _ but I did feel better about myself and like I fit in a little bit better at church. I continued to be a relatively good kid, get straight As, and want to be a professional baseball player when I grew up. My own experience with the sinner's prayer is often why I say I don't believe I was truly "saved" until my life started to be changed by my faith later in high school.

Part of the reason I started to take my faith seriously in high school is because my youth pastor didn't think of youth group as just a fun place to hang out with other students, eating pizza and playing dodgeball. We did all of those things (none of which are bad), but I thank God that my high school youth pastor saw our youth group as a means of theological education, not just as a means of manufacturing moral students before they left for college.

Pastors and church leaders: if we want to equip believing Millennials in our churches for God-glorifying lives of ministry, we must understand the importance of theological education and take the steps necessary to equip Millennials with a deep knowledge of and abounding love for God.

THE IMPORTANCE OF THEOLOGICAL EDUCATION AMONG MILLENNIALS

This chapter is the first in the final section of this book, which is about how pastors and church leaders might equip believing Millennials for gospel ministry. The two chapters that follow this one may be more practical than this, but equipping Millennials for gospel ministry must start with theological education because without a deep knowledge of God, gospel ministry is impossible.

Peter writes in 1 Peter 3:15, "But in your hearts regard Christ the Lord as holy, ready at any time to give a defense to anyone who asks you for a reason for the hope that is in you." Pastors and church leaders are, according to Ephesians 4:11, tasked with equipping the saints for ministry _ not for *doing* all of the ministry, but *equipping* people to do ministry. The cornerstone of equipping the saints for ministry is giving them a knowledge of and love for God. John Piper writes in the introduction to his book *Think* that the goal of life is to show how glorious God is and that the way this is done is, "by knowing him truly, by treasuring him above all things, and by living in a way that shows he is our supreme treasure."[28] The term "theological education" may sound dry and boring, but really all it means is "learning about who God is and what he has done." Unfortunately, recent surveys of evangelical beliefs show us that theological education is lacking among evangelicals in general, not just Millennials.

In 2016 LifeWay Research _ together with Ligonier Ministries _ released their State of Theology study. This was the second of such studies conducted with Ligonier. The results of the study are staggering, and there is much to analyze, but perhaps most concerning are some of the beliefs held by evangelicals. For instance: 72 percent of Americans with evangelical beliefs believe "Jesus was the first and greatest creature created by God." He was not the first creature created by God; he has always existed and was not created. Now, surely some percentage of Christians affirming that Jesus was the "first and greatest creature created by God" is simply because people read the question too fast. It would be easy to skim this question and think, "Of course Jesus is the greatest being to exist," not realizing that the question says "created by God." So, that may be why this number is so high. But still, this number is *really* high—too high to simply be because some people misread the question.

Further, 37 percent of Americans with evangelical beliefs believe "God will always reward true faith with material blessings." This statement sounds like the prosperity gospel and runs contrary to what the Bible teaches about those who follow Christ. Now, upon first glance, this number may seem encouraging: only 37 percent of American Evangelicals believe in a form of the false, heretical prosperity gospel. The number could be (and likely is, in some parts of the world) much higher.

But this statistic is not encouraging to me because only 25 percent of *all Americans* believe that God will always reward true faith with material blessings. This means that more "Americans with Evangelical Beliefs" believe in the prosperity gospel than "all Americans." This is not surprising, in some sense, but it is sad nonetheless. These are just two examples of poor theological education among American evangelicals.

Obviously, theological education is important for all generations—not just Millennials. But this is chapter is about equipping *Millennials* in your church for gospel ministry. So, why is theological education important to Millennials specifically?

It is important to equip Millennials in your church with a deep knowledge of God because it is the cornerstone of the gospel ministry they are called to do as followers of Jesus. Further, Millennials interact daily with peers who doubt the basic tenets of the Christian faith at a higher rate than any generation who has come before them. According to the Pew Research Center's recent Religious Landscape survey, approximately 87 percent of Baby Boomers believe in

"God" with some certainty, whereas only about 75 percent of Millennials believe the same. Millennial Christians need theological education so that they can 1) have an intimate knowledge of and relationship with God, and 2) share the gospel with their friends. And, as Paul writes in Ephesians 4:11, church leaders are to equip the saints for ministry. But, how should pastors and church leaders practically equip Millennials with a deep knowledge of and love for God?

THREE PRACTICAL WAYS TO EQUIP MILLENNIALS WITH A DEEPER KNOWLEDGE OF GOD

Most pastors and church leaders would agree that Millennials, and Christians in general, could use more theological education. If you are reading this book, you likely understand the importance of having a deeper knowledge of and love for God. But, sometimes, practically taking steps to educate people about who God is and what he has done can be sort of difficult. If you want to equip Millennials in your church, you may be unsure of the best way to approach them because you are unsure of how they would best learn. Here are three ways I have seen pastors and church leaders effectively approach theological education with Millennials.

OFF-CAMPUS SMALL GROUPS

When it comes to groups ministry in a church, small groups that meet on location at the church tend to have higher attendance than small groups that meet off campus in homes—this is not always the case, but it is common. However, while they may not be as well attended in some contexts, off-campus groups that meet in someone's home, for instance, tend to feel less formal because of their location and may promote more quality discussion and be more welcoming to newcomers to the group.

We'll dig deeper into effective Millennial community in the next chapter, but in terms of learning together, meeting off campus may be the best place to. Perhaps you want to have a sort of church book club in which you read and discuss timely (or timeless) theological works in a coffee shop or home once per month. Meeting outside of the church building will likely be more comfortable for the Millennials in your church and any friends they may bring. If they are more comfortable, they may be more likely to open up and generate good discussion.

My most formative discipleship moments have happened amidst the ambient noise of coffee shops or in the quiet of people's homes, not under the buzzing fluorescent lights of a Sunday school classroom. So, I'm biased, but I think off-campus groups are most effective when it comes to Millennial theological education.

THE TRADITIONAL SUNDAY SCHOOL SETTING

Another setting in which you could approach theological education with Millennials is the traditional Sunday school setting. While many Millennials—myself included—may prefer the informal setting of a coffee shop or home, there is nothing wrong with doing theological education in the context of the church Sunday school classroom. Like I said above, it is likely that you will have a higher attendance in this setting because people are more accustomed to showing up at a church on a Sunday morning than they are someone's house on a Thursday night, for instance.

In 2014 Eric Geiger wrote about the benefits of gathering together in the church instead of outside the church for groups ministry.[29] The benefits of gathering in the church include, but are not limited to, having built-in programs for children and having a clear stop/start time. So, while it may not be the most preferred option among many Millennials, gathering to teach theology in the church building on a Sunday morning does have its benefits.

MIDWEEK SEMINARY-STYLE CLASSES

Most churches have a midweek ministry of some sort. The most common setup I have seen is the church offering several programs for all ages on a Wednesday night, almost like a second opportunity for Sunday school, but on Wednesday night instead of Sunday morning. This is a great time to have a theology class for the Millennials in your church. Maybe on Sunday mornings you prefer to engage with a traditional curriculum like The Gospel Project, Explore the Bible, or Bible Studies for Life, but in your midweek ministry you have more flexibility. You could even create basic homework assignments for your group to complete before they return the next week to give them the opportunity to engage with the material outside of your meeting. A midweek class walking through a systematic theology text or doing an in-depth study on a book of the Bible is a great opportunity to equip the Millennials in your church with the theological education they need to share the gospel of Jesus with a world in need.

THEOLOGICAL EDUCATION FOR
GREAT COMMISSION WORK

Pastors and church leaders: you must equip the Millennials in your church with the theological education they need to do Great Commission work. This can look different in different contexts: some churches will prefer off-campus, informal meetings; other churches will prefer more formal meetings in the church either on Sunday mornings or in the middle of the week. Regardless of how, where, or when you choose to do it, *you must do it*. Ephesians 4:11 is clear: church leaders equip the saints for ministry. Believing Millennials in your churches are hungry for the knowledge of God; do not deprive them of the opportunity to learn as much as possible. Whether you're investing in Millennials one by one in one-on-one settings or in larger groups, you are instructed to equip them. In fact, equipping Millennials with the tools to do gospel ministry is going to be one of your most effective means for reaching more unbelieving Millennials in your community because you can send the believing Millennials in your church out into the community to reach their peers.

Before you continue to the next chapter, set this book down and decide what you will do in the next week to begin equipping the Millennials in your church with a deeper knowledge of God, if you aren't doing this already. If you aren't sure how, pray and ask the Lord to give you wisdom.

8/ **LIVE TOGETHER**

The most transformative three years of my life were my junior and senior years of high school and my freshman year of college. Though I prayed the sinner's prayer when I was in the fourth grade, I often cite my junior year of high school as when I actually became a Christian. It was not until then that the gospel changed my heart and that I started living for God's purposes instead of my own. What made those three years of my life so transformative? The gospel is *what* transformed my heart, as it continues to do, but in those three years, solid Christian community is *how* the gospel transformed my heart.

Many events over the course of those three years changed me: everything from broken relationships to applying to college to fixing those broken relationships. But the one constant, especially in my junior and senior years of high school, was the presence of gospel community in my life.

Our youth group had a number of small groups that met throughout the week at different leaders' homes. At the beginning of my junior year of high school, I was invited to join the small group led by my youth pastor, Phil. This small group was made up of both boys and girls and consisted of about fifteen_twenty students. For some this is too big to be a "small group," but for us it worked very well. It never felt like anyone was left out or unengaged. If anything, I was one of the quieter students, and as you'll see, the group profoundly impacted me.

A couple of parts about this small group were particularly transformative for me in the moment and even now, many years later, as I often think back to this group as a great example of gospel community.

First, the most powerful part of this small group experience was the one-on-one meetings we had once per week outside of the group. Each week, we were not allowed to leave our Monday night small group until we had paired up with someone of the same sex to meet with before we returned to small group the next Monday night. The purpose of the weekly one-on-one meetings was to hold each other accountable, but not in the sort of quasi-Catholic-confessional way a lot of people do accountability, where you meet with someone to list all the ways you've sinned in the last week. This accountability was different. We met one on one with each other to discuss the Scripture we had been assigned to read in the last week, and through that conversation about the Scripture we would often confess sin to one another, and we always concluded by praying for one another. All of this as high school students! These hour-long, one-on-one meetings changed my life, and they gave me lifelong friendships built on what Christ did for us, not what we could do for each other.

Second, through these weekly one-on-one meetings, I came to understand how gospel-centered community is more than just a Christian buzzword; it is a life-changing force. Our rag-tag group of high school students that met at Phil's house on Monday night had nothing in common but our belief in Jesus and the fact that our parents went to the same church. Our group was made up of video-game nerds, jocks, band geeks, confident students, insecure students, popular kids, and unpopular kids. Many of us had nothing in common, and if we had only known each other through school, we would have never spoken to each other. But because we had our belief in the gospel in common and because we met with one another outside of group once per week over coffee or dinner and poured our hearts out to one another, our community was unshakable. The gospel is what brought us together and is that upon which we built our friendship and community. It changed my life.

Now, you may be wondering, "Why has this guy rambled on for nearly seven hundred words about his high school small group?" It's a fair question.

This chapter is about the importance of gospel community in the lives of the believing Millennials in our churches. The story of how my high school small group changed my life is not meant to instruct youth pastors about how to do community; rather, it is meant to illustrate how Christian Millennials like me thirst for community founded not upon common interests that may change but on the unchangeable gospel of Jesus. As a young, high school Millennial, my life was changed by community founded on what Christ did for us, not what we could do for each other. Gospel-believing Millennials in our churches long for this kind of community. Don't deny them of it. Provide it for them.

THE CHURCH IS MEANT TO BE A FAMILY

Back in chapter 4 I wrote about Millennial institutional distrust. It affects how they view the government, the church, the institution of marriage, and more. Because of this, it is important to be sure that the local church feels more like a *family* than an *institution*. But making the local church feel more like a family than an institution is important beyond just preference. It is important to make the local church feel more like a family than an institution because it *is* more of a family than an institution.

God is clear in his Word: family is more than those who are our blood relatives. The global church, the body of Christ, is the family and household of God. In Mark 3 a crowd approaches Jesus and tells him that his mother and brothers are seeking him. Jesus responds by asking, "Who are my mother and my brothers?" and continues by answering his own question, "Whoever does the will of God is my brother and sister and mother." Jesus is, obviously, not dismissing the family system altogether, for if he did that he would be undermining the Scriptures that detail one's relationship with parents, widows, and others. But Jesus clearly identifies "family" as more than those who are related to us by blood or marriage.

First Timothy 3 is riddled with examples of how the church is the "household of God." Overseers and deacons must manage their own households well because, as Paul says in verse 5, "If anyone does not know how to manage his own household, how will he take care of God's church?" Paul writes in verse 15, ". . . I have written so that you will know how people ought to conduct themselves in God's household, which is the church of the living God, the pillar and foundation of the truth."

The Scripture is clear: the church is the family of God. But, the implications of this truth are not so clear. Dietrich Bonhoeffer writes in his classic *Life Together*, "Christian brotherhood is not an ideal which we must realize; it is rather a reality created by God in Christ in which we may participate."[30] Indeed, but what does it look like to participate in it? Well, on a local-church level, it can look any number of ways. Let's break it down into three categories: spiritual, emotional, and physical.

First, the local church family cares for the spiritual needs of one another. Brothers and sisters in Christ pray for one another. In prayer, we have the privilege to enter the throne room of God and communicate with him our failures, our needs, our hurts, and our fears. We must use this privilege for the good of our brothers and sisters in Christ—we must pray for *them*. Further, we should be keeping each other accountable for sin and for pursuing Christ-likeness. If our "accountability" is nothing more than admitting sin to a friend, we miss out on the opportunity to keep each other spiritually accountable in other ways.

Keep each other accountable by committing to meet with a small group member each week to talk about what you have been reading in Scripture. If you forget to pray for one another on your own, have a Saturday morning prayer meeting in someone's home now and then. Being brothers and sisters in Christ, we must care for one another spiritually, and this care must be more than just keeping each other from sin—but it should *at least* be that.

Second, the local-church family cares for the emotional needs of one another. Caring for the spiritual needs of one another is a no-brainer, but this one is sometimes overlooked. Life can be lonely. Life can be scary. Life can be depressing. Caring for one another spiritually can certainly address these realities, but caring for each other emotionally is important too. Christians are family, but we should also be friends!

Carve time out of your busy week to share a meal with others in your small group, host game nights at your home, and schedule playdates for your kids. Caring for our Christian family emotionally is an extension of caring for one another spiritually. We share time together, get to know each other better, and support each other amidst the tumultuous circumstances life throws at us.

Third, the local church family cares for the physical needs of one another. This one is pretty straightforward, isn't it? When a storm blows through and a tree falls on your small group leader's house, go help clean it up. When a small group member is diagnosed with cancer and has to travel for treatment, take care of their kids. When your prayer partner has a baby, set up a plan for people to take the family meals for a few weeks. Christians are called to care for the physical needs of one another.

The church is the family of God. We are all adopted as sons and daughters of the Father God by the faith we have in the finished work of the Son of God. Because of our adoption, we care for each other as a family spiritually, emotionally, and physically. The local church is a familial community built upon the finished work of God in Christ. What does this mean for Millennials, though? How do Millennials view community?

MILLENNIALS LONG FOR COMMUNITY

In March 2017 PBS *NewsHour* interviewed Casper ter Kuile, an irreligious researcher from Harvard Divinity School, about how Millennials are interested in spiritual matters but not in traditional religious community settings. Casper says that Millennials are disregarding traditional religious congregations because they "don't appeal to him," and that he's not alone—a high percentage of Millennials are doing the same. Casper says that he has found "countless examples" of

Millennials finding new ways to create community that fulfill the same functions a religious community has, but without the religion. Some examples he lists are CrossFit, Afro Flow Yoga, and simply sharing a meal together. He says, "You may dismiss these communities as simple entertainment, but we're convinced that this is the new face of religious life in America."

Casper's right. His equation of a local church and Cross-Fit or yoga is unfortunate and inaccurate from our evangelical perspective, but in the eyes of many Millennials, finding community in a Sunday morning Afro Flow Yoga class is not really all that different from finding community in a local evangelical church_in fact, from their perspective, it's *better* because their yoga friends don't judge people like they believe a local evangelical church would.

For many Millennials, community alone, even if that community is built upon the superficial foundations of workouts or meals, is what provides the transcendent experience their souls so desperately seek.

For many Millennials, the community *is* the end. The feeling of belonging to something greater is derived simply from hanging out with more than one person. "Greater" is almost used as a quantitative term, not a qualitative one. Even at its best, non-Christian Millennial community does community service work that might be "something greater," but it is ultimately temporary.

For Christians, community *is not* the end itself. The feeling of belonging to something greater is actually derived from *belonging to something greater*, something *better*, something *eternal*. Unfortunately, what irreligious Millennials do not understand is that communities built around yoga mats or dinner tables cannot parallel Christian communities because, while they may look similar, their foundations are different—their reasons for meeting are different.

The foundation for an irreligious Millennial community is the shared interests in food or workout regimen. The foundation of an evangelical Millennial community is the gospel of Jesus Christ, and this community simply works itself out around dinner tables or church buildings. Millennials have their problems, and it's fair to call them out on those. But when it comes to how they want to do church, Millennials' preferences align with much of what we see in the New Testament. Just two examples are Acts 2 and Galatians 6. In both chapters the local church functions more like a loving family than a rigid institution. Acts 2 shows us what it looks like when a church is drawn to repentance and generous giving so that it might be unified in its pursuit of Jesus. Galatians 6 encourages Christians to bear one another's burdens and to persist in doing good for the benefit of those in the faith.

So what does gospel-centered community look like? Gospel-centered community is built on the gospel (duh), but the gospel is a complex reality that has multiple facets and countless implications.

TWO FOUNDATIONS OF GOSPEL-CENTERED COMMUNITY

First, gospel-centered community is built on sacrifice. The heart of the gospel is sacrifice. The good news is that Christ gave himself up for the sins of the world. Jesus Christ lived the perfect life we can't live and died the horrible death we should have died so that, by his sacrifice, we can live with God forever. What does this sacrifice look in our church community, though? Does it mean we should be giving our lives for people? Possibly, but obviously that's not very common.

Gospel-centered community requires us to sacrifice our time, our money, our emotions, our homes, our hobbies, and a host of other things we might rather keep to ourselves.

Gospel-centered community looks like sacrificing your time on a Saturday to help someone in your small group move, taking up money to help pay for a car for a single mother in the church, or hosting a missionary on furlough for a couple of months. All of this sounds uncomfortable, and that's because gospel-centered community does not prioritize comfort. Gospel-centered community, being built on the gospel, is characterized by the sacrificial love, not by the toleration of selfishly maintaining personal comfort.

Gospel-centered community is not natural for many of us because our sinful hearts prevent us from wanting to care about others more than ourselves. We must rely on the sanctifying power of the Holy Spirit to empower us to maintain the selfless, sacrificial love for others that gospel-centered community requires. This is no easy feat, and it requires much prayer.

Second, gospel-centered community is built on unconditional love. Next to sacrifice, nothing is more central to the gospel than love. Really, they are quite related. The unconditional love of God is what ultimately led him to sacrifice his Son to pay for the sins of the world. This love is unconditional because it is not based upon who we are or what we do. In the same way, as we think about gospel-centered community and what it might look like in our churches, gospel-centered community does not love conditionally. Our love for those in our church or in our small group must not be based upon what others can do for us. It must be rather based upon what Christ has done for us and for them. This sort of unconditional love means we cannot be content with each other discovering our "own truth" or doing whatever we think is right. This sort of unconditional love requires us to spur one another on to holiness (Heb 10:24). We must love one another so deeply that we grieve when we see a brother or sister in Christ run astray of the gospel.

It's pretty clear how we show this love to others: we love people no matter who they are or how they differ from us. Furthermore, unconditional love must withstand disputes and fights within the church community. The church is made up of a bunch of sinners, and the sin that involuntarily oozes out of our mouths and our hands will inevitably burn others like radioactive acid. When such filth and pain accompany Christian community, the temptation is to bail on the local church. We must not do this.

Christ died on the cross for the people spitting at him *and* the people praying for him. We ought to love our community enough to endure its sins. Christ loved us enough to save us from our sin by dying on a cross constructed in sin. We ought to love each other enough to forgive and love as he has.

If we are to benefit from the sacrificial love of gospel-centered community, we must also love sacrificially for the sake of our community. This can be burdensome. Sacrificial love is rarely easy_after all, it is *sacrificial*. But, by the grace of God, sacrificial love brings joy in its wake. Loving others as Christ has loved us is a worshipful, God-glorifying experience.

COMMUNITY IS A GRACIOUS GIFT OF GOD

The church is the family of God. Living in community as the family of God requires the presence of the Holy Spirit because, in our sin, it is difficult to love others with the sacrificial, unconditional love with which Christ has loved us. However, despite the inevitable imperfection of our Christian community, it is necessary and, ultimately, a gracious gift of God. Bonhoeffer writes in *Life Together*, "Where Christians live together the time must inevitably come when in some crisis one person will have to declare God's Word and will to another."[31]

Regardless if our churches have no Millennials or our churches have only Millennials, we must provide the familial community of co-laborers who can proclaim God's Word and will to those who need it in the everyday routine of life and in their time of deepest need. Millennials have ideas about community, and pastors and church leaders should be aware of those. But, ultimately, the Scripture shows us that the sacrificial, unconditional love of Christ undergirds our community no matter how it works itself out practically in the ministry of our churches.

9/ **SERVE TOGETHER**

D uring high school, I went on two short-term mission trips to San Juan, Dominican Republic. I know
that high school short-term mission trips sometimes get a bad rap for being more akin to tourist
trips, but the two trips I went on were personally transformational, and I think the Dominican families with whom we
interacted benefited from our being there as well. The trips
didn't consist of much: we just organized a vacation Bible

school program for one of the barrios in San Juan and did some construction work on the compound where we were staying. Some of the work we did served the native people of San Juan and some benefitted the long-term missionaries stationed in the town and other groups like our own who would pass through the compound throughout the year. We didn't reach unreached people groups in remote mountain ranges or translate the Bible into a new language, but we did learn what it meant to set aside our own comforts and desires for the good of our teammates, the locals in the barrios, and, ultimately, for the kingdom of God.

This trip was personally transformational for me because it made me realize how deeply selfish I am in a way I never understood before. It wasn't the poverty of the locals that made me feel this way—they seemed perfectly happy even though they lived in cinderblock huts and had few personal items—it was the interaction with my own teammates that alerted me to my selfishness and sin. Helping the locals by leading the vacation Bible school program was personally rewarding to be sure, and much appreciated by the families in the area, but the simple act of serving others showed me how much I would prefer to serve myself and myself alone. These trips convicted me of my own self-centeredness like no other experience quite had. What those mission trips and other experiences like them have taught me is that there are social justice issues that require me to put aside my own pursuits in order to help others. Many Millennials feel this same conviction, regardless of their faith or the lack thereof.

MILLENNIALS: THE ACTIVIST GENERATION

Millennials are social activists in a way generations before them have not been. According to a 2014 study conducted by advertising agency TBWA Worldwide, seven out of ten Millennials identify as "social activists."[32] Likewise, according to a report called "The Civic and Political Participation of Millennials" published by the non-partisan thinktank New America, 53 percent of Millennials favor an "activist government," which is a higher percentage than any other generation.[33] In a similar study conducted in 2013 by Cone Communications, Public Relations, and Marketing, 36 percent of Millennials reportedly investigated the business practices and social issues supported by companies, compared to just 29 percent of the overall population.[34]

These are just statistics, though. If we pay attention to the world around us, it becomes quite clear that Millennials are activists. Take note of any major social justice movement in the last few years—Students for Life, Black Lives Matter, and more other movements like these were largely led by, or comprised of, Millennials. While many of the social justice issues with which Millennials are involved may often be broadly categorized as more "liberal" in nature, especially those not rooted in the local church, they are justice efforts nonetheless. For Millennials who would categorize themselves as religious "nones" and who are not participating in the life of the local church, social justice is ultimately rooted in a sort of fundamental moral care for their fellow man. Ultimately, this faithless social justice terminates in itself—the final purpose is to care for the felt needs of the ones for whom justice is being sought. This is a noble pursuit, and one about which Christians should care. But pursuing social justice for justice's sake is ultimately only a temporary fix for an eternal person made in the image of a God they don't know, who has given them a salvation they aren't aware they need.

Pastors and church leaders, the Millennials in our churches whom we are trying to equip with tools to be ministers of the gospel care deeply for the welfare of other people. The desire for social justice is not a desire that we will need to awaken in their hearts. They already have the motivation. They just need the guardrails to keep them on the road of doing gospel-centered social justice so as not to fall into the ditches of gospel-less social justice or a social-justice-less gospel.

SOCIAL JUSTICE WITHOUT THE
GOSPEL IS INCOMPLETE

For a long time, especially in America, the church was divided regarding social justice work. One group of Christians believed the church must pursue social justice concerns and did so without proclaiming the gospel. Another group of Christians believed the church must only concern itself with the salvation of souls and not get caught up in activism and social justice matters. This is perhaps an oversimplification of the battle between the two ideologies, but it will do for this book.

A recent book addresses the relationship between social justice and the gospel with poise. Andy Crouch deals with the pretty-much-done-but-still-sometimes-active battle between Christians over the balance of social justice work and gospel proclamation in his book *Playing God*. He writes, "What both sides have gradually (and sometimes grudgingly) realized is that care for the poor and oppressed, and proclamation of the good news of salvation through Jesus, simply are both essential biblical themes."[35] He goes on to explain that both the proclamation of the gospel and social justice are means to their respective ends. The proclamation of the gospel is the means to the end of the restoration of the relationship between God and man, and social justice is the means to the end *shalom*, "that rich Hebrew word for peace," he writes, "describing the conditions where every creature can be fully, truly, gloriously itself."[36]

Indeed, the proclamation of the gospel and the good work of seeking justice for our fellow humans are compatible. For that reason, the Christian must not pursue social justice apart from the proclamation of the gospel. Justice is a noble, worthy pursuit, but it addresses a temporary problem, and one worth addressing. However, social justice without the gospel is incomplete because it doesn't tell the whole story. When our hearts stop beating in our chests and our bodies begin decaying in our graves, the injustice of the world will give way to the justice of God. Face to face with the justice of God, we have but one hope, and that is the grace of God. Pursuing social justice for those around us is ultimately less about alleviating pain and suffering and is more about human flourishing. Crouch addresses this in his book as well when he says that by pursuing justice without the gospel, we are ultimately just replacing one set of gods with another.

So, one potential ditch on the road to equipping the Millennials in our churches to be activists is focusing on social justice without emphasizing the gospel. This creates an ultimately incomplete and eternally unfilling form of social justice. The other ditch, however, is just as troublesome.

THE GOSPEL WITHOUT SOCIAL
JUSTICE IS INCONCEIVABLE

While one group of Christians may be more prone to the error of pursuing social justice without the gospel, the other group will be prone to proclaiming the gospel with no consideration for its social justice implications. Amidst the controversy between Christians who did social justice work and Christians who simply proclaimed the gospel in the mid-twentieth century, theologian Carl Henry praised evangelicals who were pursuing biblical justice in his 1946 work *Uneasy Conscience of Modern Fundamentalism*. These evangelicals were pursuing a sort of middle ground in which the gospel would be proclaimed to people and justice would be sought for people, while so many Christians did one without the other.

In reality, proclaiming the gospel without also caring about social justice is inconceivable. It just doesn't make any sense. J. P. Callahan writes in the *Evangelical Dictionary of Theology* that there is good reason for Christians to find constructive ways to pursue justice in their communities while at the same time keeping themselves at an arm's distance from the "dominant culture." He writes, "The influence of the gospel modifies both the rationale and practice of citizenship, responsibility within culture and family, primarily through a uniquely Christian identity."[37] When a Christian has been radically changed by the gospel of Jesus Christ, a desire for peace, *shalom*, for everyone is a natural outcropping of gospel transformation.

Some of you may be nervous about pursuing social justice because it may require you to partner with people in your community who do not vote how you vote or believe what you believe. Crouch speaks to this in his book as well. He says, "We can work for common goals for uncommon reasons."[38] Indeed, democrats and republicans and Muslims and Christians can all work together to eradicate orphans or homelessness in a given community. It *is* possible. Ultimately, our reasons for pursuing justice will be different, but what justice looks like may not be.

Believing the gospel without also fighting social injustice is inconceivable. Christ himself says in Mark 12 that the two greatest commandments are: 1) love the Lord with all our heart, soul, mind, and strength, and 2) love our neighbor as ourselves. Even Jesus does not separate the love of God and love of neighbor—the two are intimately related. Finally, one last quote from Crouch sews this up well. He writes at the end of his section on the relationship between evangelism and social justice, "Because idolatry and injustice are the twin fruits of the curse, the work of evangelism and the work of justice are one."[39]

Pastors and church leaders, the Millennials in our churches have a heart for serving people who are hurting—they are the "activist generation." Some of them, though, may not best know how to pursue justice while proclaiming the gospel. At the same time, some of them may be passionate about sharing the gospel but are unsure how to seek justice in their community. Proclaiming the gospel and seeking justice are meant to be together, not separated, and we have the opportunity to lead the Millennials in our churches to pursue a biblical social justice that promotes human flourishing with eternity in mind.

But, what are some practical ways we can equip Millennials to live on mission in our communities and around the world? Here are three basic steps to take.

THREE WAYS CHURCHES EQUIP MILLENNIALS TO LIVE ON MISSION

PRAY FOR THEM

Trying to send Millennials out of our churches to live on mission without properly petitioning God on their behalf is foolishness and will ultimately prove frustratingly unfruitful. Pastors and church leaders, we must pray first for ourselves, that the Lord would give us the wisdom to lead the Millennials in our churches to pursue gospel-saturated social justice.

Likewise, we need to pray for the Millennials we're leading. Pray that the Lord would warm their hearts to serve others if they are still uneasy. Pray that these Millennials would avoid the pitfalls of a social-justice-less gospel or a gospel-less social justice. Pray that the Lord will give guidance on what social justice pursuits would be best for your particular context. Injustice exists everywhere and in all kinds of ways, so it can be hard to discern where to start. In prayer, the Lord can provide guidance on what needs may be most urgent or appropriate given the gifts of the ones being sent out to do gospel work. In short, the Lord can provide wisdom, guiding the kind of work we send people out to do.

No missional effort, however well intentioned, can be successful without first petitioning the Lord in prayer. Ask for wisdom; ask for courage; ask for guidance. Trying to do the work of God apart from the wisdom of God is foolish.

FUND THEM

Almost all missional work, whether in our local communities or in faraway lands, require money to be spent in some form or fashion. If you want to provide food for the homeless, you're going to need to buy food. If you want to adopt every orphan in your county, you're going to have to pay for fees and forms. If you want to take the gospel to unreached people groups in the Himalayas, you're going to have to purchase plane tickets. Pastors and church leaders, a lot of Millennials in our churches simply do not have much money. Many of them may not have enough money to feed themselves well, let alone feed others. An important part of equipping the Millennials in our churches to serve their communities or groups of people on the other side of the globe is helping them raise the funds they need to do so.

Fundraising can look any number of ways. Conduct a church-wide garage sale to which church members can donate items with all of the money being donated to the service effort. Gather odd jobs that need done from church members like landscaping or home cleaning that the Millennials can do in exchange for a donation to the mission trip or community service project. Ask church members to donate food items for the homeless service project instead of expecting the Millennials doing the work to go out and buy all the food themselves.

A lack of funds should never prevent gospel work in our local communities or on the other side of the world. But, pastors and church leaders, we may need to think strategically to help the Millennials we're sending out get the funding they need to do the gospel work they plan to do.

COMMISSION THEM

Finally, after praying for the Millennials we're equipping for missional work and securing the funding they need to do the work, we must *send them out*. Sending these Millennials out to live on mission will look different for different contexts. Whether we're sending Millennials out to share the gospel with the people of Ghana or announcing the start of a homeless ministry in the local community, we should commission the Millennials we're sending in front of the church. Gather the Millennials at the front of the church sanctuary, lay hands on them, pray for them, ask God's blessing on them. This is important for a number of reasons, but the act of the church commissioning the group of believers to go out and do gospel work under the banner of Christ is powerful because it communicates to the ones being sent that they are not going alone—the church stands behind them to support them in any way they can.

Those whom the church sends out to do work on behalf of the kingdom of God are not sent alone. With them they take the Holy Spirit and the prayers and support of the local church who has sent them. Pastors and church leaders, as we equip Millennials for gospel service, whatever form that takes, commission them in front of the church so that the church may be reminded to pray for them and so that the ones being sent may be reminded that they do not go out alone.

REDEEMING MILLENNIAL ACTIVISM

In the past, Western Christians have been split over the relationship between social justice work and gospel proclamation. What a tragedy! The pursuit of justice and the proclamation of the gospel were never meant to be pitted against each other. Pastors and church leaders, as we seek to equip the Millennials in our churches for gospel ministry, we have the opportunity to take the desire for justice that resides in the hearts of Millennials and give it a healthy, God-glorifying gospel orientation. Do not neglect or fear the justice-seeking hearts of the young people in your churches. Pray for them, support them, and commission them for the good of the world and the good of the kingdom of God.

MOVING FORWARD

Writing a book like this is difficult because, while ministering to Millennials will be important until the last one dies, it feels as though the recent interest in Millennials is already waning. Over the last eight-or-so months it's taken to write this book, the subject material has sometimes felt more irrelevant with each passing day.

At least one book has already been published on ministering to Generation Z, those who fill children's ministries today. Is ministering to Millennials already blasé, irrelevant, and not quite retro enough to be cool? I don't believe so.

My hope is that, assuming you are reading this chapter after all of the others (like one properly reads a conclusion) you feel as though ministering to those born between 1980 and 2000 is as relevant as ever.

Why?

Because gospel ministry is never irrelevant_even if you're just paying particular attention to a small section of people.

Throughout this entire book my goal has been to give you a bit of insight into the Millennial generation so that your sharing of the gospel with them and your equipping of them might be even more effective. The gospel of Jesus Christ alone can save unbelieving Millennials and make them look more like Jesus. My prayer is that this book is a complementary tool, a brief cultural overview, to the gospel ministry you're already doing.

3 STEPS TO BETTER UNDERSTAND MILLENNIALS

KEEP AN OPEN MIND

For Gen Xers and Boomers, the temptation is to adopt a sort of "get-off-my-lawn" posture toward Millennials that oozes phrases like, "Those kids are on their phones all the time" or "Maybe they should just move out of their parents' basement." I beg you, Gen Xers and Boomers, keep an open mind about Millennials and how they choose to live their lives. I'm not asking you to endorse a Millennial's choice to mooch off his parents. I am simply asking you to not pass judgment too soon. Before you criticize an entire generation of people because a 20-something cut you off in traffic, take a moment to pause and gather yourself.

When a young man in your church talks about living with his parents, don't assume it's because he's lazy. When a young woman in your church talks about delaying marriage until she has achieved some career goals, don't think she is irresponsible. When Gen Xers and Boomers pass hasty judgments on Millennials because they aren't reaching adulthood in the same way their parents or grandparents did, nothing is accomplished and walls are constructed.

Don't compromise the truth, but keep an open mind, being slow to pass judgment.

DO YOUR RESEARCH

Believe it or not, this is not the definitive book on the Millennial generation.

Shocking, right?

If you're interested in studying Millennials from a distance, as more of a sociological pursuit than an interpersonal one, I suggest many books to you. Below are just a few.

Read everything Dr. Christian Smith of Notre Dame writes on Millennials and faith, such as *Souls in Transition* and *Lost in Transition*. Dr. Smith's books are not exclusively about "Millennials," but the young people he is interviewing for the books are Millennials, so all of his work is in bounds when it comes to Millennial research.

Be sure to read Dr. Thom and Jess Rainer's book *The Millennials*. The data in the book is a bit dated now, but it is the first book I read on the generation, so I have to recommend it. It is, like I hope this book is, an accessible guide to the entire generation. Their book focuses more on helping you understand the generation. It was written for a broader audience than just Christians, so they don't talk much about ministry.

The last book I will recommend (I could recommend many more) is *The Next America* by Paul Taylor of the Pew Research Center. The book is based largely off the *Millennials in Adulthood* study I have cited throughout this book. Instead of asking you to read the study and the raw data, which I would only wish on someone as nerdy as I am, I suggest you read Taylor's book, which makes the data in that massive study more accessible.

INVEST IN A MILLENNIAL OR THREE

No step to understanding Millennials will be as rewarding or effective as this one. You can do all the research you want, keeping an open mind and not bemoaning the quirks of Millennials, but nothing will be as effective as *actually interacting* with one.

Contrary to common stereotypes, Millennials do not detest authority figures. They tend to be more skeptical of authority figures than previous generations, but that doesn't mean they don't respect and value the investment of their elders. Find a Millennial or three in your local church or in your neighborhood and invest in them. The honest truth is that you may be more intimidated by them than they are of you. We really can't expect to understand people unlike us until we invest time with them in real life.

God has given us in Christ a Great Commission to make disciples far and wide, baptizing them in the name of God for his glory. When God gave us the Great Commission over two thousand years ago, he knew that Millennials would arise and that you would be reading this book right now. God is not surprised that young Americans are ditching religion, nor is he concerned. God knows that, by the Spirit, we will obey his Great Commission and make disciples of these young people. God is not overwhelmed by the increasing secularization of American youth, and we shouldn't be either.

3 STEPS TO REACH UNBELIEVING MILLENNIALS WITH THE GOSPEL

PRAY FOR AN OPPORTUNITY

The three steps to reaching an unbelieving Millennial with the gospel are not unique to reaching Millennials, but they certainly apply. Before you wring your hands and get anxious about sharing the gospel with a Millennial, spend time before God in prayer. Ask the Lord to give you the courage to share your faith and the wisdom to answer any questions the Millennial you encounter may have for you. Any evangelistic pursuit that is not bathed in prayer is bound for fruitlessness.

RELY ON THE HOLY SPIRIT

I am not as prolific an evangelist as I hope to be, but when I do share my faith with others, I am amazed at how the Holy Spirit guides my words and blesses my conversation. I have only ever led a few people to Christ, but even in gospel conversations I have had that may seem discouraging in the moment, the Holy Spirit has given me the words to say and the courage to say them.

After you have prayed and asked the Lord to be with you in your sharing of the gospel, trust that the Holy Spirit will truly be your helper and guide your words.

PRESENT THE GOSPEL

Nothing about the Millennial generation voids the life-changing power of the gospel of Jesus Christ. Even if we stumble over our words and look like complete fools in the process of telling someone about Jesus, God uses the good news through our weaknesses. My prayer is that this book helps you present the gospel humbly and with great clarity to a generation of people in dire need, but I know that if you just share the gospel, the Lord can work.

3 STEPS TO EQUIP BELIEVING MILLENNIALS TO LIVE GREAT COMMISSION LIVES

HELP THEM KNOW GOD

Biblical illiteracy is a serious, cross-generational problem in the local church. In order for the Millennials in our churches to live Great Commission lives, they must think rightly about God and his Word. The local church's task is to equip them with a right knowledge of God so that they may serve him, sharing the gospel and loving their neighbors. In order for Millennials to go to the nations, making and baptizing disciples, they must have an intimate knowledge of the God they serve. The local church must equip them in this way.

HELP THEM KNOW THEMSELVES

This is an underrated part of local church ministry, I think. We are often too afraid to think of ourselves for fear of falling in love with ourselves. But if the Millennials in our churches are going to live lives of Great Commission purpose, they must have a keen awareness of their strengths and weaknesses. Pastors and church leaders, as we consider how we might equip Millennials in our churches for lives of gospel ministry, consider how you can help these young people do a bit of introspection and understand themselves better. A proper identification of one's strengths and weaknesses is important, even for the others-focused lifestyle required by a follower of Jesus Christ.

LET THEM LOOSE

Send out your young people! Whether you are sending Millennials halfway across the globe to reach an unreached people group with the gospel or you're sending them halfway across the state to plant a new church in a different town, equip your Millennials and send them out to do gospel ministry elsewhere. Building our own little kingdoms of local church ministry is often a vain pursuit. We sometimes hesitate to send people out to plant churches or serve as missionaries because we're afraid of hurting attendance numbers or losing money. We can't be fearful of what might happen if we send our Millennials out. We have to trust the Lord to bless our churches as sending churches.

MY PRAYER FOR YOU

Millennials are not the future of your church. Disciples are the future of your church. My prayer for you as you finish this book and go about doing ministry is that you will not be so concerned with Millennials that others in your church are neglected. I pray that you will use what you have learned in these pages in supplement to the Scriptures and the gospel ministry you are already doing. Do not be captivated by the urgent need to reach Millennials at the expense of others in your church. Likewise, do not neglect the urgent need to reach Millennials out of fear or frustration. Pray, trust the Lord to guide you by his Spirit, and make disciples of all nations and all ages, baptizing them in the name of the Father, Son, and Holy Spirit.

ACKNOWLEDGEMENTS

I dedicated this book to my wife because of the remarkable impact she has on every day of my life, but truly, this book could have been dedicated to a dozen people, including my incredible parents, Joe and Catherine.

I began studying Millennials after reading *The Millennials* by Thom and Jess Rainer the summer after my sophomore year of college. I had no idea who Thom Rainer was at the time. He wrote the foreword to this book, and I am blessed to serve the church under his leadership at LifeWay. Thanks to Thom and Jess for the book that inspired me to begin studying Millennials more than five years ago.

I read Trevin Wax's blog throughout college, and I didn't realize he worked at LifeWay until we happened to sit at the same lunch table shortly after I arrived in Nashville in 2013. This book would not have been possible if Trevin would not have started mentoring me in 2014. He told me that he thought pastors needed a theologically conservative Millennial to help them reach Millennials. So, he helped me launch Millennial Evangelical in May 2014, which is what led to this book. Trevin, your friendship and wisdom have made me more like Jesus.

Big shout out to the folks who edited individual chapters I assigned them because of their expertise. Trillia Newbell, Trevin Wax (again), Aaron Earls, Bob Smietana, Marty Duren, Barnabas Piper, Brandon Smith, Michael Kelley, and Dan Darling, your edits were invaluable. Thank you.

Finally, I have to thank one last person: Mr. John Houser, my freshman and sophomore English teacher. At Snider High School, in Mr. Houser's freshman English class, we had to turn in a three-to-four-page essay every week for the entire semester. It changed my life. To be developed as a writer at such a young age was transformative. I would be unfit to write a single blog post if it weren't for the investment Mr. Houser made in me as a punk high school kid. I don't know if he'll ever read this, but if so, thanks Coach Houser.

ABOUT THE AUTHOR

hris Martin (M. Div., Southeastern Baptist Theological Seminary) is a Content Strategist at LifeWay Christian Resources. Chris started *MillennialEvangelical*.com in May 2014 to help pastors and church leaders better understand, reach, and equip Millennials. He and his wife Susie live outside of Nashville, TN, with their dog, Rizzo.

— ENDNOTES

[1] There is no universal agreement as to the precise years that bracket the Millennial generation, so we will broadly define it as 1980-2000 as do many research organizations.

[2] As with the Millennial range, I have generalized the range of Baby Boomers and Gen Xers into 20-year increments for the sake of simplicity. This is not as precise as some may like, but that's OK.

3   Pew Research Center, *Millennials: Confident. Connected. Open to Change.*, 5.

4   Pew Research Center, *Millennials in Adulthood*, 6.

5   Ibid.

6   William Frey, "Diversity Defines the Millennial Generation," Brookings Institution, June 28, 2016, Accessed April 7, 2017, https://www.brookings.edu/blog/the-avenue/2016/06/28/diversity-defines-the-millennial-generation/.

7   Ibid.

8   Rick Warren, *The Purpose Driven Life: What on Earth Am I Here for?* (Grand Rapids: Zondervan, 2002), 265).

9   Brené Brown, *The Gifts of Imperfection: Let Go of Who You Think You're Supposed to Be and Embrace Imperfection* (Center City, MN: Hazelden, 2010), 50.

10 Charles Taylor, *A Secular Age*, (Cambridge, MA: Harvard University Press, 2007), 475.

11 Ibid.

12 Public Religion Research Institute, *How Race and Religion Shape Millennial Attitudes on Sexuality and Reproductive Health*, 2.

13 Ibid.

14 Awakened Man. November 21, 2013. Accessed September 18, 2017. https://www.youtube.com/watch?v=_bKQXmvdr8o.

[15] Ed Stetzer and Chris Martin, "Nominals to Nones: 3 Key Takeaways from Pew's Religious Landscape Survey," The Exchange | A Blog by Ed Stetzer, May 12, 2015, Accessed September 18, 2017, http://www.christianity-today.com/edstetzer/2015/may/nominals-to-nones-3-key-takeaways-from-pews-religious-lands.html.

[16] Michael Lipka, "Millennials Increasingly Are Driving Growth of Nones," Pew Research Center, May 12, 2015, Accessed April 12, 2017, http://www.pewresearch.org/fact-tank/2015/05/12/millennials-increasingly-are-driving-growth-of-nones/.

[17] Christian Smith with Melinda Lundquist Denton, *Soul Searching: The Religious and Spiritual Lives of American Teenagers* (Oxford: Oxford University Press, 2009), 162.

[18] Christian Smith and Melinda Lundquist Denton, *Soul Searching*, 162-162.

[19] Pew, *Millennials in Adulthood*, 4.

[20] Harvard University, "No Front-Runner Among Prospective Republican Candidates, Hillary Clinton in Control of Democratic Primary, Harvard Youth Poll Finds," Harvard IOP at The Kennedy School, Accessed May 1, 2017, http://iop.harvard.edu/no-front-runner-among-prospective-republican-candidates-hillary-clinton-control-democratic-primary.

[21] Pew, *Millennials in Adulthood*, 7.

22   Lipka, "Millennials."

23   Andrew Murray, *Humility* (Fig, 2012), 1-2.

24   Ibid., 7.

25   Ibid., 23.

26   Rose Kreider and Renee Ellis, "Number, Timing, and Duration of Marriages and Divorces: 2009," U.S. Census Bureau, May 2011, Accessed May 5, 2017, https://www.census.gov/prod/2011pubs/p70-125.pdf

27   Simon Sinek, *Start with Why: How Great Leaders Inspire Everyone to Take Action* (London: Penguin), 45.

28   John Piper, *Think: The Life of the Mind and the Love of God* (Wheaton, IL: Crossway, 2011), 15.

29   Eric Geiger, "Trade-Offs on Where Your Groups Meet," *EricGeiger.com*, March 11, 2014, Accessed September 18, 2017.

30   Dietrich Bonhoeffer, *Life Together*, (New York: Harper One, 2009), 30.

31   Bonhoeffer, 105.

32   TBWA, "The Future of Social Activism," Accessed March 11, 2017, http://www.tbwaperu.com/cultura/the-future-of-social-activism/.

33   Hollie Russon Gilman and Elizabeth Stokes, "The Civic and Political Participation of Millennials," New America, 2014, Accessed March 22, 2017, https://www.newamerica.org/documents/1752/

The_Civic_and_Political_Participation_of_Millennials. pdf, 58.

[34] CONE Communications, "2013 CONE Communications Social Impact Study," October 1, 2013, Accessed May 3, 2017, http://www.conecomm.com/ research-blog/2013-cone-communications-social-impact-study#download-research, 58.

[35] Andy Crouch, *Playing God: Redeeming the Gift of Power* (Downers Grove, IL: InterVarsity, 2013), 79.

[36] Ibid, 80.

[37] J. P. Callahan, "Gospel, Social Implications Of," *Evangelical Dictionary of Theology*, 2nd ed., edited by Walter Ewell, (Grand Rapids: Baker Publishing, 2001), 561.

[38] Crouch, 84.

[39] Ibid.